Be prepared...
To learn...
To succeed...

Get **REA**dy. It all starts here. REA's preparation for the NJ ASK is **fully aligned** with the Core Curriculum Content Standards adopted by the New Jersey Department of Education.

Visit us online at
www.rea.com

READY, SET, GO!®

NJ ASK
Language Arts Literacy
Grade 6

With REA's TestWare® on CD-ROM

Frank Stebbins

Language Arts Instructor

Kumpf Middle School

Clark, New Jersey

Research & Education Association
Visit our website at
www.rea.com

*The Performance Standards in this book were created and implemented
by the New Jersey State Department of Education. For further information,
visit the Department of Education website at www.state.nj.us/njded/cccs.*

Research & Education Association
61 Ethel Road West
Piscataway, New Jersey 08854
E-mail: info@rea.com

Ready, Set, Go!®
New Jersey ASK
Language Arts Literacy
Grade 6
with TestWare® on CD-ROM

Printed in the United States of America

Library of Congress Control Number 2009937720

ISBN-13: 978-0-7386-0514-2
ISBN-10: 0-7386-0514-X

Windows® is a registered trademark of Microsoft Corporation.

Contents

About Our Author

Frank Stebbins graduated *cum laude* from Seton Hall University, East Orange, New Jersey, with a Bachelor of Science in Education. He also holds a master's degree in Educational Leadership from Walden University, Minneapolis, Minnesota. Mr. Stebbins has been a classroom teacher since 2002 and has taught language arts and social studies classes in grades 4 through 8. He has also developed 6th, 7th, and 8th grade writing curriculums.

In 2007, Mr. Stebbins was the recipient of the *Governor's Teacher of the Year* award for his district and has been the recipient of multiple grants that promote student writing outside of traditional classroom assignments.

About Research & Education Association

Founded in 1959, Research & Education Association (REA) is dedicated to publishing the finest and most effective educational materials—including software, study guides, and test preps—for students in elementary school, middle school, high school, college, graduate school, and beyond.

Today REA's wide-ranging catalog is a leading resource for teachers, students, and professionals.

We invite you to visit us at *www.rea.com* to find out how "REA is making the world smarter."

Acknowledgments

We would like to thank REA's Larry B. Kling, Vice President, Editorial, for supervising development; Pam Weston, Vice President, Publishing, for setting the quality standards for production integrity and managing the publication to completion; John Cording, Vice President, Technology, for coordinating the design and development of REA's TestWare®; Diane Goldschmidt, Senior Editor, for project management, editorial guidance, and preflight editorial review; Alice Leonard, Senior Editor, for post-production quality assurance; Christine Saul, Senior Graphic Artist, for cover design; Heena Patel, Technology Project Manager, for design contributions and software testing efforts; and Rachel DiMatteo, Graphic Artist, for her design contributions and post-production file mapping.

We also gratefully acknowledge S4Carlisle Publishing Services for page design and typesetting.

Chapter 1
Succeeding on the NJ ASK6 Language Arts Literacy Test

ABOUT THIS BOOK AND TESTWARE®

This book , along with REA's exclusive TestWare® software, provides excellent preparation for the New Jersey ASK6 Language Arts Literacy Assessment. Inside you will find lessons, drills, strategies, and practice tests—all with a single-minded focus: success on the NJ ASK6, an acronym that stands for Assessment of Skills and Knowledge.

We have made every effort to make the book easy to read and navigate. The practice tests are included in two formats: in this book and software package.

There are **two lesson sections:**

Chapter 2 teaches the reading skills that the test will assess. This chapter starts off with a basic summary of the skills that will be reviewed and a reminder of the importance of following directions. This is followed by helpful hints on how to answer questions regarding vocabulary, main ideas, the organization of the reading passage, and the interpretation of the author's meaning. After these skills are introduced, narrative and informational texts are provided for you to practice answering sample questions.

Chapter 3 focuses on improving your ability to use the writing process to complete persuasive and speculative prompts. The section focuses on prewriting, preparing a written response, and proofreading that response. The lessons will help improve and expand your existing knowledge of these areas.

Finally, this book concludes with **two full-length practice tests** to give you a realistic test experience of the NJ ASK6 test before the actual test. Following each test, answers and complete explanations are provided.

We recommend that you begin your preparation by first taking the practice exams on your computer. The software provides timed conditions and instantaneous, accurate scoring that makes it easier to pinpoint your strengths and weaknesses.

HOW TO USE THIS BOOK AND TESTWARE®

FOR STUDENTS: The best way to prepare for a test is to practice, and you'll find that we've included drills with answers throughout the book, and that our two practice tests include detailed answers. You'll find that our practice tests are very much like the actual ASK6 you'll encounter on test day.

In addition, prepare for the test by reading over the test information and study tips. Take practice test 1 on CD-ROM to determine your strengths and weaknesses, and then study the course review material, focusing on your specific problem areas. The course review includes the information you need to know when taking the test. Make sure to follow up by taking practice test 2 on CD-ROM so you're thoroughly familiar with the format and feel of the NJ ASK 6 Language Arts Literature Assessment.

FOR PARENTS: New Jersey has created grade-appropriate standards for English language arts and has listed them in clusters, which are explained below. Students need to meet these standards as measured by the ASK6. Our book will help your child review for the ASK6 and prepare for the Language Arts Literacy exam. It includes review sections, drills, and two practice tests complete with explanations to help your child focus on the areas he or she needs to work on to master the test.

FOR TEACHERS: No doubt, you are already familiar with the ASK6 and its format. Begin working through each of the lessons in succession. When students have completed the subject review, they should move on to the practice tests. Answers and complete answer explanations follow each of the practice tests.

WHY STUDENTS ARE REQUIRED TO TAKE THE NJ ASK6

In 1996 the New Jersey State Board of Education adopted Core Curriculum Content Standards that define New Jersey's expectations for student learning. The board updated the Language Arts Literacy standards in 2004. To determine how well a student is advancing and whether the student is on course to perform well in high school, sixth grade students are required to take the ASK6.

The ASK is one of the key tools used to identify students who need additional instruction to master the knowledge and skills detailed in the Core Curriculum, the standards that guide education in New Jersey.

WHAT'S ON THE NJ ASK6

By the time a student enters the sixth grade, he or she will be experienced at taking standardized tests. Starting from the third grade, the NJ ASK is given annually until a student enters high school. The test has been derived from the same set of expectations that are given to teachers from which to create their lesson plans.

The sixth-grade version of the test was revised for the 2007/2008 school year. Currently, the test contains two days of language arts assessment including reading passages and writing prompts. The test is usually given in May and all students are required to take it. The reading portion contains two narrative passages with related questions. Questions will include multiple-choice questions ranging from vocabulary skills to comprehension-based topics. For each reading passage, students are also required to complete an open-ended response. Students will be given 40 minutes to work on the passages. The informational, everyday reading passage will make up 30 minutes of the test. For the writing portion, students will complete persuasive and speculative prompts. Persuasive prompts will be answered in 45 minutes while the speculative prompts will be answered in 25 minutes.

All questions are based on ASK6 language arts literacy content clusters and skills, which are outlined in the following table.

New Jersey Core Curriculum Content Standards	Related Content found in Practice Test 1 at:	Related Content found in Practice Test 2 at:
STANDARD 3.1 (Reading) All students will understand and apply the knowledge of sounds, letters, and words in written English to become independent and fluent readers, and will read a variety of materials and texts with fluency and comprehension.		
3.1.6.A. Concepts About Print/Text		
2. Survey and explain text features that contribute to comprehension (e.g., headings, introductory, introductory, concluding paragraphs).	Day 1 and Day 2 Sections 1 and 3	Day 1 and Day 2 Sections 1 and 3
3.1.6.C. Decoding and Word Recognition		
2. Use context clues or knowledge of phonics, syllabication, prefixes, and suffixes to decode new words.		Day 1 Section 1, # 3 Section 3, # 3 and 7 Day 2 Section 1, # 4 Section 3, # 5
3. Apply knowledge of new words correctly (refer to word parts and word origin).		Day 1 Section 1, # 3 Section 3, # 3 and #7 Day 2 Section 1, # 4 Section 3, # 5
4. Apply spelling and syllabication rules that aid in decoding and word recognition.		Day 1 Section 1, # 3 Section 3, # 3, and 7 Day 2 Section 1, # 4 Section 6, # 5

3.1.6.D. Fluency		
1. Adjust reading speed appropriately for different purposes and audiences.	Day 1 and Day 2 Sections 1 and 3	Day 1 and Day 2 Sections 1 and 3
3. Read silently for the purpose of increasing speed, accuracy, and reading fluency.	Day 1 and Day 2 Sections 1 and 3	Day 1 and Day 2 Sections 1 and 3
3.1.6.E. Reading Strategies (before, during, and after reading)		
1. Activate prior knowledge and anticipate what will be read or heard.	Day 1 and Day 2 Sections 1 and 3	Day 1 and Day 2 Sections 1 and 3
2. Vary reading strategies according to their purpose for reading and the nature of the text.	Day 1 and Day 2 Sections 1 and 3	Day 1 and Day 2 Sections 1 and 3
3. Reread to make sense of difficult paragraphs or sections of text.	Day 1 and Day 2 Sections 1 and 3	Day 1 and Day 2 Sections 1 and 3
4. Make revisions to text predictions during and after reading.	Day 1 and Day 2 Sections 1 and 3	Day 1 and Day 2 Sections 1 and 3
3.1.6.F. Vocabulary and Concept Development		
1. Infer word meanings from learned roots, prefixes, and suffixes.		Day 1 Section 1, # 3 Section 3, # 3 and 7 Day 2 Section 1, # 4 Section 3, # 5
2. Infer specific word meanings in the context of reading passages.		Day 1 Section 1, # 3 Section 3, # 3 and 7 Day 2 Section 1, # 4 Section 3, # 5

3.1.6.G. Comprehension Skills and Response to Text		

1. Respond critically to an author's purpose, ideas, views, and beliefs.		Day 1
		   Section 3, # 6
		Day 2
		   Section 3, # 8

3. Use cause and effect and sequence of events to gain meaning.		Day 1
		   Section 1, #1, 5, and 9
		   Section 3, # 5
		Day 2
		   Section 1, # 2

4. Construct meaning from text by making conscious connections to self, an author, and others.	Day 1 and Day 2 Section 1, # 10; Section 3, # 10	Day 1 and Day 2 Section 1, # 10 Section 3, # 10

6. Recognize and understand historical and cultural biases and different points of view.		Day 1
		   Section 3
		Day 2
		   Section 3, # 3

7. Identify and analyze features of themes conveyed through characters, actions, and images.		Day 1
		   Section 1, # 6
		Day 2
		   Section 1, # 5
		   Section 3, # 7

8. Distinguish between major and minor details.		Day 1
		   Section 1, # 5
		Day 2
		   Section 1, # 6

9. Make inferences using textual information and provide supporting evidence.		Day 1
		   Section 1, #1, 5, 7, 8, 9, and 10
		   Section 3, #4, 6, 8, and 10
		Day 2
		   Section 2, # 7 and 10
		   Section 3, #1, 2, 3, 6, 9, and 10

12. Recognize characterization, setting, plot, theme, and point of view in fiction.		Day 1 Section 1, #1, 2, 4, 5, 6, 7, and 8 Section 3 #1 Day 2 Section 1, #1, 2, 3, 5, 6, 7, 8, and 9 Section 3, #1, 2, 3, 6, 7, and 9
13. Recognize sensory details, figurative language, and other literary devices in text.		Day 1 Section 3, #2 and 9 Day 2 Section 3, # 4

3.1.6.H. Inquiry and Research		
1. Develop and revise questions for investigations prior to, during, and after reading.	Day 1 and Day 2 Sections 1 and 3	Day 1 and Day 2 Sections 1 and 3

STANDARD 3.2 (Writing) All students will write in clear, concise, organized language that varies in content and form for different audiences and purposes.

3.2.6.A. Writing as a Process (prewriting, drafting, revising, editing, postwriting)		
1. Write informational compositions of several paragraphs that engage the interest of the reader, state a clear purpose, develop the topic, and conclude with a detailed summary.	Day 2 Section 2	Day 2 Section 2
2. Generate ideas for writing through reading and making connections across the curriculum and with current events.	Day 1 and Day 2 Section 1, # 10 Section 2 Section 3, # 10	Day 1 and Day 2 Section 1, # 10 Section 2 Section 3, # 10
3. Expand knowledge about form, structure, and voice in a variety of genres.	Day 1 and Day 2 Section 1, # 10 Section 2 Section 3, # 10	Day 1 and Day 2 Section 1, # 10 Section 2 Section 3, # 10

4. Use strategies such as graphic organizers and outlines to elaborate and organize ideas for writing.	Day 1 and Day 2 Section 2	Day 1 and Day 2 Section 2
5. Draft writing in a selected genre with supporting structure and appropriate voice according to the intended message, audience, and purpose for writing.	Day 1 and Day 2 Section 2	Day 1 and Day 2 Section 2
6. Make decisions about the use of precise language, including adjectives, adverbs, verbs, and specific details, and justify the choices made.	Day 1 and Day 2 Section 1, # 10 Section 2 Section 3, # 10	Day 1 and Day 2 Section 1, # 10 Section 2 Section 3, # 10
7. Revise drafts by rereading for meaning, narrowing focus, elaborating and deleting, as well as reworking organization, openings, closings, word choice, and consistency of voice.	Day 1 and Day 2 Section 1, # 10 Section 2 Section 3, # 10	Day 1 and Day 2 Section 1, # 10 Section 2 Section 3, # 10
9. Review and edit work for spelling, usage, clarity, organization, and fluency.	Day 1 and Day 2 Section 1, # 10 Section 2 Section 3, # 10	Day 1 and Day 2 Section 1, # 10 Section 2 Section 3, # 10
12. Understand and apply the elements of a scoring rubric to improve and evaluate writing.	Day 1 and Day 2 Section 2	Day 1 and Day 2 Section 2
3.2.6.B. Writing as a Product (resulting in a formal product or publication)		
1. Expand knowledge of characteristics, structures, and tone of selected genres.	Day 1 and Day 2 Section 1, # 10 Section 2 Section 3, # 10	Day 1 and Day 2 Section 1, # 10 Section 2 Section 3, # 10

2. Write a range of grade-appropriate essays across curricula.	Day 1 and Day 2 Section 1, # 10 Section 2 Section 3, # 10	Day 1 and Day 2 Section 1, # 10 Section 2 Section 3, # 10
3. Write grade-appropriate, multi-paragraph expository pieces across curricula.	Day 1 Section 2 Day 2 Section 5	Day 1 Section 2 Day 2 Section 5
5. Support main idea, topic, or theme with facts, examples, or explanations, including information from multiple sources.	Day 1 and Day 2 Section 1, # 10 Section 2 Section 3, # 10	Day 1 and Day 2 Section 1, # 10 Section 2 Section 3, # 10
6. Sharpen focus and improve coherence by considering the relevancy of included details, and adding, deleting, and rearranging appropriately.	Day 1 and Day 2 Section 1, # 10 Section 2 Section 3, # 10	Day 1 and Day 2 Section 1, # 10 Section 2 Section 3, # 10
7. Write sentences of varying length and complexity, using specific nouns, verbs, and descriptive words.	Day 1 and Day 2 Section 1, # 10 Section 2 Section 3, # 10	Day 1 and Day 2 Section 1, # 10 Section 2 Section 3, # 10
9. Provide logical sequence throughout multi-paragraph works by refining organizational structure and developing transitions between ideas.	Day 1 Section 2 Day 2 Section 5	Day 1 Section 2 Day 2 Section 5
10. Engage the reader from beginning to end with an interesting opening, logical sequence, and satisfying conclusion.	Day 1 and Day 2 Section 1, # 10 Section 2 Section 3, # 10	Day 1 and Day 2 Section 1, # 10 Section 2 Section 3, # 10

3.2.6.C. Mechanics, Spelling, and Handwriting		
1. Use Standard English conventions in all writing, such as sentence structure, grammar and usage, punctuation, capitalization, spelling, and handwriting.	Day 1 and Day 2 Section 1, # 10 Section 2 Section 3, # 10	Day 1 and Day 2 Section 1 # 10 Section 2 Section 3, # 10
2. Use a variety of sentence types and syntax, including independent and dependent clauses and prepositional and adverbial phrases, to connect ideas and craft writing in an interesting and grammatically correct way.	Day 1 and Day 2 Section 1, # 10 Section 2 Section 3, # 10	Day 1 and Day 2 Section 1, # 10 Section 2 Section 3, # 10
3. Use knowledge of English grammar and usage to express ideas effectively.	Day 1 and Day 2 Section 1, # 10 Section 2 Section 3, # 10	Day 1 and Day 2 Section 1, # 10 Section 2 Section 3, # 10
4. Use correct capitalization and punctuation, including commas and colons, throughout writing.	Day 1 and Day 2 Section 1, # 10 Section 2 Section 3, # 10	Day 1 and Day 2 Section 1, # 10 Section 2 Section 3, # 10
5. Use quotation marks and related punctuation correctly in passages of dialogue.	Day 1 and Day 2 Section 1, # 10 Section 2 Section 3, # 10	Day 1 and Day 2 Section 1, # 10 Section 2 Section 3, # 10
6. Use knowledge of roots, prefixes, suffixes, and English spelling patterns to spell words correctly in writing.	Day 1 and Day 2 Section 1, # 10 Section 2 Section 3, # 10	Day 1 and Day 2 Section 1, # 10 Section 2 Section 3, # 10
7. Demonstrate understanding of reasons for paragraphs in narrative and expository writing and indent appropriately in own writing.	Day 1 Section 1, # 10 Section 2 Section 3, # 10 Day 2 Section 1, # 10 Section 3, # 10	Day 1 Section 1, # 10 Section 2 Section 3, # 10 Day 2 Section 1, # 10 Section 3, # 10

8. Edit writing for correct grammar usage, capitalization, punctuation, and spelling.	Day 1 and Day 2 Section 1, # 10 Section 2 Section 3, # 10	Day 1 and Day 2 Section 1, # 10 Section 2 Section 3, # 10
10. Write legibly in manuscript or cursive to meet district standards.	Day 1 and Day 2 Section 1, # 10 Section 2 Section 3, # 10	Day 1 and Day 2 Section 1, # 10 Section 2 Section 3, # 10
3.2.6.D. Writing Forms, Audiences, and Purposes (exploring a variety of forms)		
1. Write for different purposes (e.g., to express ideas, inform, entertain, respond to literature, persuade, question, reflect, clarify, share) and a variety of audiences (e.g., self, peers, community).	Day 1 and Day 2 Section 1, # 10 Section 2 Section 3, # 10	Day 1 and Day 2 Section 1, # 10 Section 2 Section 3, # 10
2. Gather, select, and organize information appropriate to a topic, task, and audience.	Day 1 and Day 2 Section 1, # 10 Section 2 Section 3, # 10	Day 1 and Day 2 Section 1, # 10 Section 2 Section 3, # 10
3. Develop and use knowledge of a variety of genres, including expository, narrative, persuasive, poetry, critiques, and everyday/workplace writing.	Day 1 and Day 2 Section 1, # 10 Section 2 Section 3, # 10	Day 1 and Day 2 Section 1, # 10 Section 2 Section 3, # 10
4. Organize a response that develops insight into literature by exploring personal reactions, connecting to personal experiences, and referring to the text through sustained use of examples.	Day 1 and Day 2 Section 1, # 10 Section 2 Section 3, # 10	Day 1 and Day 2 Section 1, # 10 Section 2 Section 3, # 10

5. Write persuasive essays with clearly stated positions or opinions supported by organized and relevant evidence to validate arguments and conclusions, and sources cited when needed.	Day 2 Section 5	Day 2 Section 5
10. Use a variety of strategies to organize writing, including sequence, chronology, cause/effect, problem/solution, and order of importance.	Day 1 and Day 2 Section 1, # 10 Section 2 Section 3, # 10	Day 1 and Day 2 Section 1, # 10 Section 2 Section 3, # 10
11. Demonstrate higher-order thinking skills and writing clarity when answering open-ended and essay questions in content areas or as responses to literature.	Day 1 and Day 2 Section 1, # 10 Section 2 Section 3, # 10	Day 1 and Day 2 Section 1, # 10 Section 2 Section 3, # 10
13. Demonstrate the development of a personal style and voice in writing.	Day 1 and Day 2 Section 1, # 10 Section 2 Section 3, # 10	Day 1 and Day 2 Section 1, # 10 Section 2 Section 3, # 10
14. Review scoring criteria of relevant rubrics.	Day 1 Section 2 Day 2 Section 5	Day 2 Section 5 Day 2 Section 5

PREPARING FOR THE TEST

There are plenty of things students can do before and during the actual test to improve their test-taking performance. The good thing is that most of the tips described below are easy!

Test Anxiety

Do you get nervous when your teacher talks about taking a test? A certain amount of anxiety is normal, and it actually may help you prepare better for the test by getting you motivated. Nonetheless, too much anxiety is a bad thing and may keep you from properly focusing. Here are some things to consider that may help relieve test anxiety:

- Share how you are feeling with your parents and your teachers. They may have ways of helping you deal with your concerns.

- Keep on top of your game. Are you behind in your homework and class assignments? A lot of your classwork-related anxiety and stress will simply go away if you keep up with your homework assignments and classwork. And then you can focus on the test with a clearer mind.

- Relax. Take a deep breath or two. You should do this especially if you get anxious while taking the test.

Study Tips and Taking the Test

- **Learn the test's format.** Don't be surprised. By taking a practice test ahead of time, you'll know what the test looks like, how much time you will have, how many questions there are, and what kinds of questions are going to appear on the actual exam. Knowing ahead of time is much better than being surprised.

- **Read the entire question.** Pay attention to what kind of answer a question or word problem is looking for. Reread the question if it does not make sense to you, and try to note the parts of the question needed for figuring out the right answer.

- **Read all the answers.** On a multiple-choice test, the last answer could also be the right answer. You won't know unless you read all the possible answers to a question.

- **It's not a guessing game.** If you don't know the answer to a question, don't make an uneducated guess. And don't randomly pick just any answer, either. As you read over each possible answer to a question, note any answers that are obviously wrong, then select one of the remaining answers. Each obviously wrong answer you identify and eliminate greatly improves your chances at selecting the right answer.

- **Don't get stuck on questions.** Don't spend too much time on any one question. Doing this takes away time from the other questions. Work on the easier questions first. Skip the really hard questions and come back to them if there is still enough time.

- **Accuracy counts.** Make sure you record your answer in the correct space on your answer sheet. Fixing mistakes later wastes valuable time.

- **Finished early?** Use this time wisely and double-check your answers.

SOUND ADVICE FOR TEST DAY

- **The night before.** Getting a good night's rest will keep your mind sharp and focused for the test.

- **The morning of the test.** Have a good breakfast. Dress in comfortable clothes. Keep in mind that you don't want to be too hot or too cold while taking the test. Get to school on time. Give yourself time to gather your thoughts and calm down before the test begins.

TIPS FOR PARENTS

- Encourage your child to take responsibility for homework and class assignments. Help your child create a study schedule. Mark the test's date on a family calendar as a reminder for both of you.

- Talk to your child's teachers. Ask them for progress reports on an ongoing basis.

- Commend your child's study and test successes. Praise your child for successfully following a study schedule, for doing homework, and for any work done well.

- Attack test anxiety head-on. Your child may experience nervousness or anxiety about the test. You may even be anxious, too. Here are some helpful tips on dealing with a child's test anxiety:

  — Talk about the test openly and positively with your child. An ongoing dialogue can not only relieve your child's anxieties but also serve as a progress report of how your child feels about the test. When talking together, make sure your child understands what areas he or she is going to be tested on.

  — Form realistic expectations of your child's testing abilities.

  — Be a "test cheerleader." Your encouragement to do his or her best on the test can alleviate your child's test anxiety.

  — Have your child use the last days before the test to review all tested subject areas.

Chapter 2
Reading

To be successful on the reading portion of the NJ ASK6, you need to know what to expect. Each lesson found in this chapter relates to a different kind of question that may appear on the test. Questions on the test typically focus on vocabulary, finding the main idea of a passage, recognizing how literary elements are used, and making conclusions based on the text.

No matter what the question, certain tips apply. Read the tips below before starting the lessons and exercises in this chapter.

Know your time! At the beginning of each section, your teacher will tell you how much time you have. Plan accordingly. As a sixth grader, you should know how fast you are able to read. Do not rush through a section, but be certain you leave yourself enough time to answer the questions without rushing, as well as some time to check over your work.

Before reading the passage, read over the questions first. As readers, we all may find our minds drifting at times. Reading over the questions first will allow you to focus on what is important in the passage. This will be especially helpful when you need to answer the open-ended questions. As you read, look for details and information that will allow you to fully support your answers.

If words or names confuse you in the reading passage, skip over them. Sometimes proper nouns will be included in the reading passages and they may be extremely difficult to pronounce. If you find these words, do not spend too much time trying to pronounce them. Identify who or what they are, and move on.

Check your answers! Once you have finished the last question, it does not mean that you are done. If time is left, you should be looking over your answers to be sure they are exactly what you want. Make sure you have put your answers in the correct location on the answer grid, and make sure that you did not leave any blank. For open-ended questions, go back and see if you can include more details.

Do not work past the stop sign in the bottom right corner of your test booklet! If you do, your test will be voided and will not count. So, pay attention to the directions and your test booklets to avoid any possible complications.

OPEN-ENDED RESPONSES

Each of the extended reading passages will include an open-ended response for you to answer. They may not all be related to the skill being reviewed; however, all the open-ended questions will aid you in preparing for the test. The following framework should be used in answering the questions so you can prepare your best answer.

First, try to give a clear main idea statement by restating the question. From that provide 5 to 7 sentences of support. Finally, write a concluding sentence. Try not to be too creative. Save that for the speculative response in the writing section. Also, be sure to include specific information from the reading selection itself. That does <u>not</u> mean to copy word for word, though. If at all possible, include some real-life examples to support your main idea.

As with any other question, make sure you understand what you are being asked before you begin writing. Never leave an open-ended response blank. Write the best answer you can so it can earn some credit. Finally, worry more about your content than making sure every grammar mistake is taken care of. Obviously, grammar is important, but your content is more important. In the answer key, a sample response will be broken down so you can compare this with your answer.

Vocabulary

Understanding what you are reading is a crucial part of success for any subject, task, or job. Not knowing what a word means may result in having no idea what a question is asking you or having no idea what answer to select. This lesson will provide practice in:

- using context clues to create a definition

- using prefixes and suffixes plus a root word to find a definition

- formulating educated guesses to select the best answer possible

Context Clues

 **Context clues** are extremely useful tools that you can use to help with definitions on a test. These clues allow you to use the reading passage to figure out what a word means. Context clues help you to use the surrounding words or sentences to come up with a definition of the word you do not know. By using the following steps, a plan for using this strategy will be at your fingertips.

Strategy:

1. Read the sentence before and after the word.

2. Underline words that you already know in the sentences to help you form a general idea of what the sentence is talking about.

3. Using the words you underlined, create your own definition for the unfamiliar word.

4. Substitute your definition into the sentence to see if it makes sense.

Using this strategy will also give you a way to check whether or not your answer is correct. By putting your definition back into the sentence, you will be able to see if your definition is close to the actual meaning of the word. Look at the following example to see how the strategy was used.

Example 1:

The hikers had been in search of beautiful sights throughout the mountains to photograph. When they spotted the majestic bald eagle soaring above against the blue sky, they knew they found exactly what they were looking for.

— After reading this passage, you may not know the meaning of the word *majestic*. To use context clues, read the sentence before and the sentence containing the word over again.

— After the passage is reread, underline words that may help you come up with a definition.

The hikers had been <u>in search of beautiful sights</u> throughout the mountains to photograph. When they spotted the majestic bald eagle soaring above against the blue sky, they knew <u>they found exactly what they were looking</u> for.

— By looking at the underlined words, you can assume that the word *majestic* has something to do with beauty or being breathtaking.

— To check, substitute the word *breathtaking* into the sentence for *majestic* to see if it makes sense.

*The hikers had been in search of beautiful sights throughout the mountains to photograph. When they spotted the **breathtaking** bald eagle soaring above against the blue sky, they knew they found exactly what they were looking for.*

Since the definition of *breathtaking* makes sense in the sentence, you can assume that the meaning of *majestic* is close to the created definition.

Exercise 1: Context Clues

Directions: Underline the words in each sentence that help you figure out the meaning of the *italicized* word. Then use the words to create a definition. Be sure to check your definition by inserting it into the sentence and then checking the answer section at the end of the exercise.

1. After receiving the *substantial* raise, Richard was able to take his entire family on a weeklong vacation.

   Definition: _____

2. The explosion of *vivid* colors had the child explain to his mother, "The garden looks like a rainbow!"

   Definition: _____

3. The *gnarled* tree was forced to grow around the metal fence.

   Definition: _____

4. After an extremely long period without rain, the region became *arid* and unbearable to live in.

   Definition: _____

5. The people on the boat were amazed at the beautiful fish as they looked through the *translucent* viewfinder below the surface of the water.

   Definition: _____

Before checking your answers, make sure you have checked your definitions! Did you substitute each definition back into the original sentence to make sure it makes sense? If so, check your answers!

Exercise 1 Answers:

1. *substantial:* large, significant

By seeing that Richard was able to "take his entire family on vacation," you can tell that the raise he received was very big.

2. *vivid:* bright, containing a large amount of color

The words "explosion," "colors," and "rainbow" should be the context clues you underlined to help you figure out that *vivid* means something that is brightly colored.

3. *gnarled:* twisted or curved

As a result of a tree having to grow around a fence, it cannot be straight! Therefore, a *gnarled* object is one that is crooked!

4. *arid:* dry, desert-like

The context clues of "long period without rain" and "unbearable to live in" should have helped to define *arid.*

5. *translucent:* see through, clear

Since the viewfinder was placed in the water to see the fish below, the viewfinder is an object that is clear enough to see through.

Exercise 2:

Now that you have had practice in working with context clues, complete Exercise 2. This exercise is a reading passage that contains unfamiliar words just as on the NJ ASK. Use the strategies that have been discussed to help you complete this section.

To help you learn the pace at which you work, write down the time you started working on this section as well as the time you finished.

Start Time: _____

Finish Time: _____

Total Minutes: _____

Remember, a good strategy is to read the questions following the passage before you start reading! This will allow you to look for and underline context clues as you are reading. In this way, you will not waste time going back and searching through the passage. Also, before you look at any of the answer choices, try to create your own definition from the context clues. Then, match your definition to the choices on the test.

Directions: Read the following passage and answer the questions that follow.

THE RECIPE SAYS WHAT?

As Joel's mother's birthday approached, he was at a loss of what he possibly could get her. After a few days, he became <u>enlightened</u> with an idea that seemingly popped out of nowhere. He suddenly remembered how much his mother loved birthday cakes, so he decided he would bake her one.

First, he knew that he would need to gather the ingredients. After school he rode his bike to the supermarket to buy the cake mix. From the box, he quickly jotted down the ingredients and <u>rounded</u>

them up as he went up and down the aisles. By the time Joel was finished, he was almost too exhausted to ride home.

Once Joel arrived home, he knew he would have a busy night because his mom's birthday was a day away. Fighting the tiredness, Joel began to read the recipe. Much to his <u>bewilderment,</u> he was met with unknown words such as *whisk, preheat, spatula,* and multiple other cooking terms. With <u>unwavering</u> determination, Joel was not going to give up just yet!

Even though Joel thought he was taking his time, carefully examining each step of the recipe to make sure he was following it <u>precisely,</u> the kitchen became a mess of flour, sugar, and eggs. Joel began to cry seeing that the cake was a failure and that he would be left gift-less.

To his shock, his mother was standing behind him chuckling to herself. She could not believe how hard her son was working to make her a cake. Together, Joel and his mother spent the next few hours working to construct a more beautiful cake than the one on the box itself! To Joel's amazement, his mother exclaimed that this was the best birthday gift she ever received because she got to spend the entire evening with her son doing what she loved most!

For questions 1–5, fill-in the answer grid on the next page.

1. In the sentence, "After a few days, he became <u>enlightened</u> ..." the word *enlightened* means

   A. to have made brighter.

   B. to have passed time.

   C. to have been informed.

   D. to have been made sad.

2. In the passage, the word <u>rounded</u> means

   A. to have gathered up.

   B. to have made a circle around.

   C. to have smoothed the edges.

   D. to have purchased.

3. In the passage, the word <u>bewilderment</u> means all of the following except

   A. confused.

   B. dumbfounded.

   C. achieved.

   D. puzzlement.

4. In paragraph 3, the word <u>unwavering</u> means
   A. easily scared.
   B. having the quality of not giving up.
   C. being flat or smooth.
   D. annoyed when something does not work out.

5. A synonym for <u>precisely</u>, found in paragraph 4, would be
   A. messily.
   B. exactly.
   C. horizontally.
   D. carelessly.

Answer Grid: Fill in the correct circles for your answers to Exercise 2.

1.	Ⓐ	Ⓑ	Ⓒ	Ⓓ
2.	Ⓐ	Ⓑ	Ⓒ	Ⓓ
3.	Ⓐ	Ⓑ	Ⓒ	Ⓓ
4.	Ⓐ	Ⓑ	Ⓒ	Ⓓ
5.	Ⓐ	Ⓑ	Ⓒ	Ⓓ

6. Why do you think that Joel's mother commented that the cake was "the best birthday gift she ever received?" Do the best gifts always need to come in a box or be expensive?

   Use information from the story and any outside information you wish to include to support your answer.

   _____

   _____

   _____

   _____

   _____

_____

_____

_____

_____

_____

_____

_____

_____

_____

_____

Before checking your answers, be sure to go over your work to make sure all of your answers make sense in the original sentences. Also, remember to write down the time it has taken you to finish this passage. Knowing how long something takes you to read will help to make you a better test taker because you will know how to manage your time.

Exercise 2 Answers:

1. By looking at the context clues that Joel "was at a loss" of ideas, but then "one seemingly popped out of nowhere," the correct answer is C.

2. While *rounded* is a word with multiple meanings, by seeing that Joel went up and down the aisles looking for ingredients shows that the answer is A.

3. Read this question carefully. It asks you to find the word that <u>does not</u> have the same meaning. Even if you do not know what *dumbfounded* means, you know that *achieved* definitely does not make sense in the sentence. The answer is C.

4. The context clue of "determination" should have helped you come up with the answer of B.

5. Thinking about how a person would follow directions, you should come up with the answer of B.

6. Sometimes the best gift a person can receive from another person is time spent together. (*Restate the question.*) Joel's mother recognizes the effort that Joel has spent trying to make a cake for her. Her son knew how much she enjoyed baking and wanted to show his appreciation for all she does for him. Even though Joel's cake was not a success, his mother helped him create a fantastic finished product. (*Sentences 2 to 4 are based on conclusions a reader can make from the passage.*) Even though this gift was relatively cheap financially, it was rich in thought and love. (*Explains information in the passage.*) When my friend had a picture of the two of us framed at our favorite vacation spot for my birthday, it wasn't so much the frame that was important, but the memory of a great time we both had in the past. (*Outside information*) Even though people can often attach a price to gifts, one cannot attach a price to time spent with one another. That is the best gift in itself. (*The conclusion is the final two sentences.*)

Word Decoding

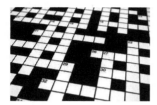 Another strategy you can use in finding the meaning of unfamiliar words is **word decoding**. This strategy involves looking at the prefix or suffix of a word and then adding that meaning to the root word to come up with a definition. Below, you will find some common prefixes and suffixes to help you complete the exercises.

Prefix	Meaning
re-	again
pre-	before
un-	not
hyper-	over
mis-	wrong

Suffix	Meaning
-tion	the act of
-able	able to
-ful	full of
-less	without
-ous	full of

Strategy:

1. Separate the unfamiliar word into the root word and the prefix/suffix.

2. Use context clues and prior knowledge to define the root word.

3. Define the prefix/suffix.

4. Add the root word and prefix/suffix together to create a definition of the unfamiliar word.

5. Check the definition by substituting it into the sentence to make sure it makes sense.

Look at the following example to see how word-decoding strategy was used.

Example 2:

When the family heard that their flight was delayed for an undetermined amount of time, they were not sure when they would be arriving home.

— After reading the passage, the word *undetermined* may be unfamiliar to you. First, you will need to break the word into its root and prefix/suffix.

> *un* is the prefix
> *determine* is the root
> *d* is the suffix

— By separating the parts, you can now work on creating individual definitions. Start with the root word.

> *determine* means to decide on something or figure it out
> *un* means not
> adding the suffix *d* to the root word changes the word to past tense

— After creating your individual definitions, add them together.

> By adding the definitions together, you get *not decided on*.

— By substituting the meaning back into the sentence, you get:

> *When the family heard that their flight was delayed for a **not decided on** amount of time, they were not sure when they would be arriving home.*

While your writing teacher would not be happy with this sentence because it is not grammatically correct, the definition does make sense. Sometimes when you are trying to create your own definitions, you should not worry as much about how the sentence sounds as much as what the sentence means.

Exercise 3: Word Decoding

Directions: For each sentence, define the *italicized* word. First separate the root word from the prefix and suffix to create individual meanings. Then, combine your meanings to create a definition for the unfamiliar word

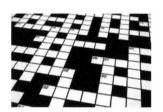

Think of this strategy like a math problem.

Prefix + Root + Suffix = Definition

1. The *unreliable* car would sometimes work in the snow, yet other times it would not even start.

    Prefix: _____

    Root: _____

    Suffix: _____

    Definition: _____

2. Because the student did not study for the geometry test, he received a *substandard* grade.

    Prefix: _____

    Root: _____

    Suffix: _____

    Definition: _____

3. The overcrowded animal shelter was a *pitiful* sight as many cages were filled with six or seven dogs.

    Prefix: _____

    Root: _____

    Suffix: _____

    Definition: _____

4. After the grizzly bear spent two months hibernating in a cave, its eyes were *hypersensitive* to the glaring sunlight as it emerged from its den.

Prefix: _____

Root: _____

Suffix: _____

Definition: _____

5. The *vigorous* hikers easily completed their five mile trek through the hills.

Prefix: _____

Root: _____

Suffix: _____

Definition: _____

Before going to check your answers, make sure you have checked your definitions! Did you substitute each definition back into the original sentence to make sure it makes sense? If so, go on to the next page and check your answers!

Exercise 3 Answers:

1. *unreliable:*
>   un: not
>   +
>   rely: to count on
>   +
>   able: able to
>   =
>   not able to be counted on

2. *substandard:*
>   sub: below
>   +
>   standard: what is expected, normal
>   +
>   no suffix
>   =
>   below expectations

3. *pitiful:*
>   no prefix
>   +
>   pity: pathetic, sad
>   +
>   ful: full of
>   =
>   full of sadness

4. *hypersensitive:*
>   hyper: over
>   +
>   sensitive: affected by, paying attention to
>   +
>   no suffix
>   =
>   overly affected by, paying too much attention to

5. *vigorous:*

no prefix

+

vigor: strength or energy

+

ous: full of

=

full of strength or energy

Exercise 4: Word Decoding

Now that you have had practice in working with context clues, complete Exercise 4. This exercise is a reading passage that contains unfamiliar words just like on the NJ ASK. Use the strategies that have been discussed to help you complete this section.

To help you learn the pace at which you work, write down the time you started working on this section as well as the time you finished.

Start Time: _____

Finish Time: _____

Total Minutes: _____

Remember, a good strategy is to read the questions following the passage before you start reading! Also, before you look at any of the answer choices, try to create your own definition by using the word-decoding strategies. Then, match your definition to the choices on the test.

Directions: Read the following passage and answer the questions that follow.

SAMANTHA'S BEST SHOT

As Samantha entered her sixth grade school year, she knew that she would be met with a number of challenges. As she adjusted to her schedule, opening her locker, and getting used to the layout of the building, she noticed a sign on the gym wall announcing soccer tryouts. While Samantha was far from an expert player, she knew that she was a <u>skillful</u> dribbler.

Samantha could hardly contain her <u>joyous</u> optimism as she rode home on the bus. She felt that her previous two years on the town's recreational team would surely give her an advantage against the other sixth graders trying out.

When Samantha entered the house, her excitement came to a screeching halt as she starting talking to Jeffrey, her <u>intolerable</u> older brother. Jeffrey told Samantha that in his three years at the middle school, he never once saw a sixth grader make the team. This bit of bad news caused her to retire to her room for a night of nervous <u>anticipation</u>.

The anticipation of the afternoon soccer tryouts caused Samantha's day to be especially <u>unbearable</u>. Finally, ninth period ended and at her locker, Samantha was faced with a decision. Even though she felt extremely nervous about trying out for the team, she did not want to go home and admit to her brother that she was scared. So, she decided that she would indeed try out.

As she arrived at the locker room, Samantha noticed something odd. She noticed that she was the only sixth grader there! At that moment Samantha knew that no matter what happened at the tryouts, she already was proud of herself for having the courage to try out.

For questions 1–5, fill in the answer grid on the next page.

1. All of the following words mean the same as <u>skillful</u> EXCEPT
    A. talented.
    B. competent.
    C. capable.
    D. hopeless.

2. Which of the following situations would cause a person to feel <u>joyous</u>?
    A. Realizing you left your lunch at home
    B. Receiving an A+ on an assignment
    C. Missing your bus
    D. Getting stuck in traffic when you are late

3. The word <u>intolerable</u> means
    A. unable to be put up with.
    B. unable to be heard.
    C. unable to be annoyed.
    D. unable to be brave.

4. <u>Anticipation</u> most closely means
   A. without warning.
   B. not being able to wait.
   C. not going fast.
   D. unable to succeed.

5. All of the following events may be considered <u>unbearable</u> EXCEPT
   A. getting detention for half an hour after school on a Friday.
   B. having to go to the dentist to have a cavity filled.
   C. going to see a concert of your favorite band.
   D. going to see your younger sister's dance recital.

Answer Grid: Fill-in the correct circles for your answers to Exercise 4.

1.   Ⓐ   Ⓑ   Ⓒ   Ⓓ

2.   Ⓐ   Ⓑ   Ⓒ   Ⓓ

3.   Ⓐ   Ⓑ   Ⓒ   Ⓓ

4.   Ⓐ   Ⓑ   Ⓒ   Ⓓ

5.   Ⓐ   Ⓑ   Ⓒ   Ⓓ

6. Why did Samantha view showing up at soccer tryouts as a huge accomplishment? How can showing up at an event be just as rewarding, if not more rewarding, than the event itself?

   Be sure to include information from the story as well as any other information you feel will support your answer.

   _____

   _____

   _____

   _____

   _____

_____

_____

_____

_____

_____

_____

_____

_____

_____

_____

_____

Before checking your answers, make sure you have checked your definitions! Did you substitute each definition back into the original sentence to make sure the meaning makes sense? If so, check your answers!

Exercise 4 Answers:

1. The correct answer is D. All of the other answers are synonyms for the word *skillful,* which means "full of skill or talent."

2. The correct answer is B. Since *joyous* means "to be filled with happiness," the only event that would cause somebody to be filled with happiness is getting an A+.

3. The correct answer is A. The prefix, *in,* means "not." *Tolerate* means "to put up with." The suffix, *able,* means "able to." Therefore, *intolerable* means "not able to put up with."

4. The correct answer is B. Anticipate means "to look forward to something happening." The suffix, *tion,* means "the act of." *Anticipation* means "the act of looking forward to something."

5. The correct answer is C. *Un* means "not" and *bearable* means "able to be put up with." *Unbearable* means "not able to be put up with."

6. Samantha was extremely proud that she was the only sixth grader to show up for soccer tryouts. Whether or not she made the team did not matter to her, because she recognized the fact that she showed courage when she just decided to try. (*Restate the question/main idea.*) Being nervous before a big event such as a championship game, final exam, or in this case, a soccer tryout, is extremely normal. Conquering this fear is not easy to do and many people are unable to actually get over this stumbling block. (*Support from passage and outside*) Samantha was most likely not the only girl in the sixth grade to play soccer. In fact, since she played for the town's team, many other girls her age actually played. But, being the one to show up showed that she had more confidence and guts than her peers. (*Explanation of support*) Just the fact that she showed up will show the coach the dedication Samantha will have for her team. Even if she does not make the team this year, Samantha will surely be a player that the coaches remember in her seventh grade year. (*Conclusions based on passage*) The reader does not know if Samantha made the team, but the reader does know that she was proud of herself. (*Restatement of the main idea.*)

READING COMPREHENSION

The following lesson will allow you to practice skills and strategies to help you understand what you are reading. By being able to break apart a reading passage, you will be able to see not only the big picture ideas the author is trying to give you, but also know why the author wrote what he or she did, as well as recognize the plot and turning points in the story. This lesson will provide practice in:

• recognizing the author's purpose for writing

• finding the main idea of a passage

• using supporting details to increase understanding of the author's message

The Author's Purpose

 One of the first things you should do when looking at a passage is to try to recognize the **author's purpose,** or reason for writing. Recognizing this will allow you to better understand the purpose behind the writing as well as the main idea of the selection.

When writing, authors have a purpose in mind. Authors hope to entertain, inform, or persuade. To entertain, a selection can tell a story or narrative about a humorous event that was witnessed or happened to the person firsthand.

Exercise 5: Author's Purpose

To get a better idea of how to recognize writing whose purpose is to entertain, complete the following activity:

List 4 topics that you would consider entertaining reading.

After completing your list, brainstorm a list of characteristics that you would find in a selection whose purpose is to entertain.

Informative pieces contain facts. They may be news articles, passages that explain how to do something, or research papers.

To get a better idea of how to recognize writing whose purpose is to inform, complete the following activity:

List 4 topics that you might find in an informative piece of writing.

After completing your list, brainstorm a list of characteristics that you would find in a selection whose purpose is to inform.

Persuasive pieces try to get the audience members to agree with the author's point of view. They might take the form of business letters or editorials to a newspaper.

To get a better idea of how to recognize writing whose purpose is to persuade, complete the following activity:

List 4 topics that you could find written in a persuasive piece of writing.

After completing your list, brainstorm a list of characteristics that you would find in a selection whose purpose is to persuade.

By having an idea of the characteristics found in each type of writing, it will be easier to answer questions regarding the author's purpose. While the topics can be quite varied, some common types and characteristics are listed below.

Writing to Entertain – Topics:	Characteristics:
How a person stood up to a bully	Dialogue
How a bad day got better	The use of "I, me, my, we" and other first-person pronouns
A story about a vacation or great experience somebody had	Main character faces a problem in the beginning of the selection and works to overcome it.
Stories about overcoming hardships	Themes of trying hard, perseverance, and never giving up

Writing to Inform – Topics:	Characteristics:
Personal Safety: How to be safe in a fire, on a bus, etc.	Facts
How to be a good student or citizen	Transitional words (first, next, then)
Information on a program such as recycling or environmental protection	Chronological order
Historical biography	Written like a recipe, directions, or instructions

Writing to Persuade – Topics:	Characteristics:
School Issues: Year-round schooling, no skateboards on school property, no cell phones in school	Opinions
Town Issues: Mandatory curfew for teenagers, save land for parks instead of building malls	Details are facts that support writer's opinions
Family Issues: Limit the number of hours a child spends on the computer or watching television	May be written as a letter
Others: Encouragement to support fundraiser, recycling, community betterment campaigns	Conclusion usually suggests that the audience do a specific action

Exercise 6: Author's Purpose

Match the story excerpts to the purpose that best describes it. Write the letter on the line following the passage.

A – To Entertain   B – To Inform   C – To Persuade

1. Being safe in one's home is something all parents, children, and people in general worry about. Homeowners can take certain precautions to adequately prepare for possible emergencies. By being prepared with a plan and the correct tools, a dangerous situation can be avoided. Having a plan is the first step. All people who live in the house should know exactly what to do in case of an emergency.

   Author's Purpose: ___

   Explanation: _____

   _____

2. As soon as I entered the tunnel, I could smell hot dogs and freshly cut grass. "Programs, peanuts, get your ice cream!" were all being shouted as we tried to find our seats. As we moved through the amazing stadium, I felt extremely tiny as the outfield fences looked miles away. Before I even saw the first pitch, I knew this would be a day to remember.

   Author's Purpose: ___

   Explanation: _____

   _____

3. Bike riding is an activity enjoyed not only by many youths, but also by many adults. As adults are often seen as role models for teenagers and elementary school children, a mandatory helmet law for all riders should be put into place. Not only would this allow adult bike riders to model proper biking etiquette, but it may also save lives.

   Author's Purpose: ___

   Explanation: _____

   _____

4. Making friends is not always easy. As a shy, only child, I was used to being around my parents most of the time. When my parents and I moved to a new town, I knew I would be in for a rude awakening. As the last days of summer flew by and the school year approached, a feeling of dread also came with the changing of the seasons.

Author's Purpose: ___

Explanation: _____

_____

5. Recycling can be achieved in numerous ways. To start a program, clearly labeled bins need to be set up in visible areas. Some label suggestions for the bins are *paper, plastic,* and *glass.* After the bins are set up, information should be made available to let people know about the program. Recycling can reduce the amount of waste in an office building by half while conserving resources.

Author's Purpose: ___

Explanation: _____

_____

 Go back and check your answers. Use the chart to look for key words that may help you identify the author's purpose. Also, make sure that your explanation completely shows why you selected your answer.

Exercise 6 Answers:

1. B. This passage is an informative piece because the paragraph seems to be introducing a set of instructions. The paragraph is introducing a plan of how to be safe in an emergency.

2. A. Because this is introducing a story about a person's experience at a baseball game, one can assume the author's purpose is to entertain.

3. C. The author's purpose is to be persuasive. The author is encouraging adult riders to wear a bike helmet and be "role models" for young riders.

4. A. Make sure that you do not confuse this with a "how-to-make friends" passage. This is a story about a person overcoming hardships.

5. B. While recycling passages often can be persuasive, this one is specifically telling you how to start a program.

Main Idea and Supporting Details

Knowing the main idea of a passage will improve your overall comprehension of that selection. The main idea is what the passage is about or the "big picture" of the writing. All information in the passage should support the main idea. The main idea may come at the beginning of the introduction or at the end of the conclusion. However, most of the time the main idea is not specifically stated, so you will have to use the supporting information of the passage to develop your own.

Recognizing supporting details will help you in a variety of ways on the NJ ASK. The recognition of details will help you with questions that ask you to distinguish between a main idea and details. Also, you can use details from the passage in the open-ended section as support for your answer.

Supporting details are those that help the author explain the main idea. Usually, sentences containing details have a variety of adjectives or facts. They may also contain the plot of a story.

To review, adjectives are words that describe nouns or pronouns. Facts are statements that can be proven true. Common examples of facts are dates, measurements, or descriptions of events that can be checked. The plot is the main part of a story. Supporting details are usually found in the body of a paragraph, essay, or passage.

A good strategy to identify supporting details or to answer questions regarding them is to identify the main idea of the passage first. To create a main idea statement, first read the entire passage. Use the introduction to get a basic idea of what the passage is about. The body of the writing will give you a great deal of information. Do not get bogged down with the minor details, but look at the message the author is trying to get across. Finally, the conclusion should summarize all the information in the piece.

Exercise 7: Main Idea and Supporting Details

To help you learn the pace at which you work, write down the time you started working on this section as well as the time you finished.

Start Time: _____

Finish Time: _____

Total Minutes: _____

Directions: Read the following passage and complete the activities that follow.

CITIZENSHIP

Many students look at their lives and wonder, "How can I make a difference in my country?" After all, students in sixth grade cannot vote, they cannot drive a car to follow traffic laws, and they do not pay most taxes. Even with all of these restrictions, students in the sixth grade can become involved in many activities to better their schools and local communities.

As a student, you can get involved in your community. At school, there are a variety of ways to do this. One way is to join a club. Some middle school clubs participate in different types of fundraisers. Some collect food or clothing for shelters, raise money to support worthy causes, or even start a recycling program. By collecting food or clothing, you can see that something that seems like a relatively small amount of effort can translate into a huge reward. Helping a family obtain the items necessary to meet their basic needs can also allow you to see how fortunate you are while you improve the life of another. Collecting financial donations can be just as useful. Throughout the school year, having drives or sales has been known to raise a significant amount of funding for heart disease, cancer, and diabetes.

Another way that you can exhibit the responsibility of citizenship is to follow the laws that apply to you. Many students walk to school or use walking as their main means of transportation. When walking, you need to be conscious of the rules of the road. Walking facing the traffic is a great way not only to ensure your safety but also the safety of drivers. Crossing at crosswalks is another great safety strategy. These same attributes apply to bike, scooter, or skateboard riders as well. An additional act of responsibility is to follow the proper safety regulations and wear a helmet. By law, a helmet is to be worn by all students in the sixth grade who bike ride. Finally, if you ride on a school bus, you should be sitting in your seat with your seatbelt securely buckled. It is impossible for a driver to focus on driving safely when passengers are running around screaming behind him or her.

It is obvious that students in the sixth grade are not able to fully participate in all of the citizenship-raising activities open to adults. However, you can show good citizenship and responsibility by using common sense and getting involved. Doing these activities at a young age can lay the foundation for you to grow into a responsible adult.

Complete the following to form the main idea of the previous section.

1. The main idea of the first paragraph is:

List any supporting details that show this.

2. The main idea of the second paragraph is:

List any supporting details that show this.

3. **The main idea of the third paragraph is:**

List any supporting details that show this.

4. **The main idea of the fourth paragraph is:**

List any supporting details that show this.

5. The main idea of the whole passage is:

6. This passage talks about the positive aspects of a middle school student taking on additional responsibilities. Analyze this information and discuss the pros and cons of getting involved in one's school.

_____

_____

_____

_____

_____

_____

_____

_____

_____

_____

_____

 Go back and check your answers. Make sure that your main idea statement clearly states the author's message. Also, make sure your supporting details provide evidence that your main idea is correct.

Exercise 7 Answers:

Responses may vary.

1. Even though sixth grade students do not have all the same opportunities to explore citizenship as adults, opportunities do exist. Details to support this main idea are found in the second and third sentences of paragraph 1.

2. Students have the opportunity to become involved in many activities that better their surrounding community while demonstrating good citizenship. Supporting details for this can involve mentioning any of the types of fundraisers or financial donation opportunities.

3. A person who obeys traffic safety laws shows good citizenship. Examples to support this statement should reference street crossing, helmet wearing, or school bus safety.

4. Quite similar to the first paragraph, the final paragraph mentions that good citizenship as a youth leads to good citizenship as an adult. The final sentence supports this statement.

5. Putting all the information together, the reader can see that the main idea in this passage is stated, and should be somewhat easy to figure out. The main idea is exactly what was stated in the first and third paragraphs. (In the next exercise, the main idea will be implied, and not directly stated.)

6. Getting involved in one's community has many rewarding aspects to it; however, it can be a rather difficult task. (*Restatement of question*) A person can feel extremely proud of efforts made to help others. (*Main idea pros*) The passage discusses various fundraisers in which a student may become involved. (*Info from passage*) Having participated in the student council's coat drive this past year, I saw what an impact a few old coats could have on another family's life. The experience was amazing. (*Outside info*) Not only did this experience get me involved in a club, but it also showed me the power citizens have when they choose to work together. (*Conclusion pros*)

    Even though getting involved can be terrific, it does come with some negative aspects. (*Main idea cons*) The more things a student becomes involved in, the less time he or she will have to focus on school work and other activities. Thinking back to the coat drive, I had to give up at least three lunch periods to set up posters, and collect and count the coats. Also, before and after school meetings created a stressful time management situation. (*Outside information*) Even though there were some definite negatives to helping out, the rewards outweighed them. I am looking forward to continuing my involvement within the student council this school year and into the future. (*Conclusion*)

Exercise 8: Main Idea and Supporting Details

To help you learn the pace at which you work, write down the time you started working on this section as well as the time you finished.

Start Time: _____

Finish Time: _____

Total Minutes: _____

Directions: Read the following passage and answer the questions. Be sure to check your work before going on to the answer section.

SIGN HERE

Are you looking for a hobby that can give you a one-of-a-kind collectable? Autograph collecting by mail can bring your favorite celebrity into your own home. While a relatively simple pastime, the rewards can be outstanding. However, caution should be taken to avoid the disappointment of a celebrity not writing back or your item being lost in the mail.

Autograph collecting is a very popular hobby that people do in person or through the mail. While in-person autograph collecting allows a fan to meet the celebrity of their choice face to face, through-the-mail collecting is a much more convenient avenue. It requires much less time than waiting for a celebrity at a talk show or movie premiere. Also, this can be done from the comfort of your own home, thus eliminating the possibility of spending time in the cold or the rain. Once you've written a letter asking for the autograph, you'll need to research the address and decide on an item to send. The only other part is anticipating the trip to the mail box.

While this sounds fun and exciting, there are a few drawbacks with this aspect of the hobby. First and foremost, not seeing the autograph signed in front of you can raise questions of authenticity. Unfortunately, many celebrities have been known to hire secretaries or assistants to respond to mail on their behalf. In addition to authenticity concerns, sometimes items are lost in the mail or they are not returned. A general rule of thumb is not to send anything you are not willing to lose.

A great bit of advice is: If you never try, you will never get anything. While there can be much excitement in collecting autographs, sometimes disappointments occur. If you are ready to take a chance, grab some envelopes, stamps, and paper, find a celebrity's address and write away!

1. All of the following are supporting details found in the third paragraph EXCEPT
   A. not seeing the autograph signed in front of you can raise questions about authenticity.
   B. you shouldn't send anything through the mail that you are not willing to lose.
   C. even though sending autograph requests through the mail can be fun, some disappointment can occur.
   D. many celebrities have been known to hire secretaries to respond to mail.

2. The main idea of the second paragraph is
   A. autograph collecting through the mail can be a fun activity.
   B. the only other part is anticipating the trip to the mail box.
   C. through the mail autograph collecting is a much more convenient avenue.
   D. the only other task that needs to be completed is researching an address to which to send the item.

3. The main idea of the entire passage is
   A. autograph collecting through the mail is a terrific hobby.
   B. because autograph collecting through the mail may result in one losing his or her favorite collectable, one should not do it.
   C. autograph collecting through the mail can bring about much excitement, but it should be done with caution as hardships may be encountered.
   D. not only is autograph collecting a fun way to pass the time, but one can also make money doing the hobby.

4. The main idea of the third paragraph is
   A. first and foremost, not seeing the autograph signed in front of you can raise questions of authenticity.
   B. in addition to authenticity concerns, sometimes items are lost in the mail or they are not returned.
   C. while this sounds fun and exciting, there are a few drawbacks with this aspect of the hobby.
   D. do not send anything through the mail you are not willing to lose.

5. Which of the following details, if added to the second paragraph, would support the main idea?

   A. The increasing price of stamps may make this hobby more difficult to enjoy.

   B. If you send a marker, make sure you put it into a bag so it does not explode on your items.

   C. Index or trading cards are inexpensive items that can easily be sent and can be built into an interesting collection.

   D. Celebrities seem much too busy to make time to open their own mail, never mind sign items for fans.

6. Celebrities often have their private lives made public. Looking back at the passage, do you think you would enjoy being a celebrity? As a celebrity, would you sign autographs for your fans? Be sure to support your answer.

_____

_____

_____

_____

_____

_____

_____

_____

_____

_____

_____

_____

_____

_____

_____

_____

_____

_____

_____

_____

_____

_____

_____

_____

Exercise 8 Answers:

1. The best way to answer this question is to figure out what the main idea of this passage is. Basically, the main idea of this passage is that autograph collecting through the mail does have some drawbacks. By reading over the answer choices, one can see that this is very similar to C. While C looks like the answer, one should still check over the others. By reading, A, B, and D, one can see that those choices all support the main idea statement, therefore, eliminating them.

2. The answer is A. The second paragraph deals with the positive and fun aspects of this hobby. All the other choices are details that explain what someone who wants to participate needs to do.

3. The answer choices need to be read carefully. Looking back at the big picture of the entire passage, one notices that it talks about both advantages and disadvantages of the hobby. The only choice that discusses both is C.

4. This question is very similar to question 1. In fact, you can use the main idea you thought of for question 1 to answer this. The answer is C. The test itself can be a tool that can assist you. Use it!

5. Looking back at paragraph 2, you can see that it deals with the positive aspects of the hobby. The only choice that mentions a positive quality is C. As you saw in this exercise, sometimes an answer letter will appear more often than others. If you feel that the answer is correct, go with it—unless of course, every answer you are getting is the same. Do not look for patterns, just look for the best possible choice.

6. Being a celebrity is not all glamorous, red-carpet events; it can also mean a lack of privacy. (*Restating the Question*) Personally, I do not think I would enjoy being a celebrity. (*Main Idea Statement*) Having paparazzi follow me everywhere, constantly doing interviews or signing autographs seems a little too overwhelming to me. (*Support*) I like peace and quiet, not having to act like everything I do is being watched. (*Explanation*)

   I think that I would sign autographs for fans under certain conditions. (*Main Idea Question 2*) If I were at a talk show or a movie premiere, I would try to sign autographs for as many people as I could. However, if I were at my home, a hotel, or with my family, I would not sign autographs. I am entitled to my own privacy just like everyone else. Finally, I do not think I would sign autographs through the mail because I would not want to be responsible for having the post office lose something that was very important to someone. (*Sentences 2 through 5 are support.*) Because of my interest in privacy, I do not feel that I would enjoy being a celebrity even though at first glance it sounds terrific. (*Conclusion*)

LITERARY ELEMENTS

 Understanding the structure of a reading passage will make it easier for you to comprehend the overall message. Most of the definitions or strategies listed in this section apply primarily to narrative passages. Narratives contain key components that make the story more clear to the reader. Grasping the message of the plot, qualities of the main characters, conflict, and solution all play a critical part in figuring out the theme or main idea being discussed.

First, you will need to know the terms that may be included in the questions. While the definitions will not be asked on the NJ ASK, the terms may be included in the questions. You cannot answer a question if you don't know what is being asked.

Conflict: a problem that occurs in the story

Plot: basically, the story being told

Main Character(s): the central figure(s) of the story

Point of View: explains who the story is being told by—the narrator is either a character in the story (first person) or the narrator is an observer outside of the story (third person)

Setting: where and when the story takes place

Solution: how the conflict or problem was solved (also referred to as the resolution)

The plot of a narrative follows a certain formula. First comes the introduction in which you usually meet one or more of the main characters. Then, as the story continues, it proceeds to explain the beginning of the conflict. Conflict can occur in a few ways:

Character vs. Himself/Herself: This occurs when a character battles to overcome a fear that he or she has within himself/herself.

Character vs. Nature: The main character has to survive the elements of nature.

Character vs. Other: This type is commonly seen and involves a character handling a given situation with another main character.

Character vs. Society: The main character deals with a situation in which he or she is pitted against views that others see as normal.

After the conflict is stated, the author develops the plot usually by describing the main character's failed attempts to solve the problem. Information on less important characters is usually found in the body of the passage, along with details that develop the main character. Next comes the climax of the story. The climax is the high point of the passage in which the character faces his biggest challenge and attempts to find a solution. Usually, this is the turning point of the reading.

After the turning point comes the conclusion. Here, the author further explains the solution, presents the theme, or provides an ending.

As with any other type of question, plan to read the questions first. Then, read the passage. This technique allows you to focus your reading on what is important and not waste time trying to interpret minor details.

Exercise 9: Literary Elements

To help you learn the pace at which you work, write down the time you started working on this section as well as the time you finished.

Start Time: _____

Finish Time: _____

Total Minutes: _____

Directions: Read the following passage and complete the activities that follow:

CONCERT BLUES

"Can you believe the concert is tonight? It seems like we were just standing in line buying tickets," I said as I talked to my friend, Steve. He agreed that time does seem to fly. Then we agreed to meet outside the arena at 7:30.

Over the course of the day, I needed to complete some tasks before I could get too excited about seeing my favorite band. First, a trip to the store needed to be made to pick up sandwiches and sodas to eat before going into the concert. At the store I ran into Mike, Carl, and Amy. I knew they all were fans of the band, so I mentioned that the concert was tonight. "You got tickets? I thought that sold out in minutes!" exclaimed an impressed Carl. The process of purchasing tickets to a concert can be an extremely frustrating and annoying experience. I knew this firsthand as I waited on line for a few hours just for the chance to get these tickets.

Since I was meeting Steve at the concert, I packed up the car and started to make my way to the arena. I knew there would be traffic, but I did not expect to be met with the bumper-to-bumper traffic that was on the highway. As people approached the arena, anyone could see that this was indeed a sold-out concert. Scalpers were on the side of the road trying to buy or sell tickets. Men were running around trying to sell passengers imitation T-shirts. Through all of this, security was trying to direct traffic into the arena parking lot.

Miraculously, after what seemed like hours staring at the trunk of the car in front of me, I pulled into the parking lot and found a spot. Immediately, I called Steve, and he met me at my car. We began to eat our sandwiches and drink our sodas.

During this time, we also began to try and guess the songs that would be played. We also decided that there would be absolutely no reason to see the opening band play. During this time, we started to walk toward the arena. As we approached the entrance, I asked Steve to give me my ticket so I could give it to security. To my dismay I heard, "Oh no! We need to go back to the car. I left the tickets there."

"No worries, we have plenty of time," I said. As we walked back to the car, worry began to creep into my stomach. I knew if he forgot the tickets, this concert experience would quickly turn into a nightmare for both of us. As we walked back I started to get a sick feeling in my stomach. When we finally arrived at his car, the frantic search began. The glove box, trunk, center console, doors, and seats were all explored hoping to find the lost treasure. Much to our dismay, the tickets were nowhere to be found. Now, I started to worry because I could not remember if I had the tickets in the first place.

Off we raced to continue the search in my car, just in case they were there. We could not believe we were going to miss the concert because we forgot the tickets. It was now too late for either of us to go home and make it back in time for the concert. The walk from his car to mine was solemn. After a quick search we realized there was nothing. Next, we were faced with the decision of whether or not to try getting tickets from scalpers, but neither of us had that kind of cash on us, especially after paying for the tickets in the first place.

Disappointment sunk in at this point. As we were about to go our separate ways I heard two fans talking. One said, "Larry, hurry up! We need to pick up our tickets at Will Call."

"That's it!" Steve yelled. "The tickets! They are at Will Call." Thinking back to the day we purchased the tickets, Steve remembered that he suggested that the tickets be kept at Will Call so nobody would lose or forget them. Unfortunately, he forgot he had to pick them up at the arena. So, without wasting any time, we raced off to the arena to pick up our tickets.

There was no line at the arena because all the fans were inside already. We finally got our tickets and went to our seats. Much to our happiness the opening band was already finished and packing up their equipment. Within ten minutes the main act began to play the first of many songs that would lead to a night of musical bliss.

1. In a sentence or two, describe the setting of the passage in your own words.

_____

_____

_____

_____

2. Who were the two main characters?

_____

_____

_____

_____

3. Using the plot, what was the main problem of the story? What type of conflict was it? Explain.

_____

_____

_____

_____

4. Explain the solution to the problem.

_____

_____

_____

_____

_____

5. What point of view is the story told in? Explain how you know.

_____

_____

_____

_____

_____

6. The passage shows that the narrator and Steve are good friends. If the tickets were not found, do you think their friendship would have been affected? Explain.

_____

_____

_____

_____

_____

_____

_____

_____

_____

_____

_____

_____

_____

_____

_____

_____

_____

_____

_____

_____

_____

_____

Exercise 9 Answers:

1. The setting takes place in modern times. The locations are an arena parking lot and briefly at a food store.

2. The two main characters are the narrator and Steve. Even though some other people were mentioned, they did not have a significant impact on the story.

3. The main problem of the story was when the tickets could not be found moments before the two friends were set to go into the arena for the concert. The type of conflict would be *Man vs. Other.* By process of elimination, the other categories can be removed leaving this one. "Other" can be a variety of events with which a main character may have difficulty.

4. The solution of the story came when two people passing by were overheard talking about picking up their tickets at Will Call. When this was heard, Steve remembered that was where the tickets were being held for that night's concert.

5. This passage is written in the first person point of view. One can tell this by observing that the narrator is an active participant in the story and interacts with the other characters.

6. If the tickets were not found by the narrator or Steve, the friendship most likely would have been the same. (*Restatement of the Question*) Details throughout the story tell that a strong friendship exists. (*Support*) It looked like this concert was planned for quite some time, and both people were looking forward to it for a while. (*Explanation*) Both friends seemed to carefully prepare for the day's events as well. (*Support*) This was seen as the narrator picked up food for that night and left early to make sure he or she arrived with enough time before the concert. (*Explanation*) Also, even though it may have been Steve's responsibility to arrive with the tickets, both characters were there when the purchase was made so it really would not have been any one person's fault. (*Support*) Even though the narrator did not physically have the tickets, it would have been a good idea to remind Steve that morning. (*Explanation*) Luckily both characters were able to enjoy the concert, but their friendship most likely would have lasted even if the tickets were not found in time. (*Conclusion*)

Exercise 10: Literary Elements

To help you learn the pace at which you work, write down the time you started working on this section as well as the time you finished.

Start Time: _____

Finish Time: _____

Total Minutes: _____

Directions: Read the following passage and answer the questions that follow.

A WALK INTO THE FOREST

Michelle and James always enjoyed hiking through the forest that was located about two miles from their house. As Saturday approached, both friends eagerly discussed which trails they would take, and some of the favorite sites they would see. "During the winter, the lack of leaves allows you to see for miles up at Lookout Point!" Michelle eagerly stated.

"I always enjoy taking the Blue Trail along the creek by the pine trees after the first snowfall. You can often see some footprints of animals in the snow," commented James.

The week at school was a drag due to the anticipation of the upcoming plans. It seemed like each day lasted a month and Saturday would never arrive. As the weekend arrived, four inches of snow fell during Friday night and into Saturday morning. When James woke up on Saturday morning, he noticed that he had a voicemail on his cell phone. The message said, "James, I know it is late, but because of the snow, I won't be able to make it back for our hike. I'm really sorry, but I went to visit my mom and I am going to stay here instead of trying to drive back. Well, if you go on your hike be careful, and make sure you bring your phone!" James was confused because he had not even bothered to look outside.

When he went to the window, he noticed that this was the perfect day for him to go hiking. Even though he was bummed that Michelle would not be around, James decided to go hiking anyway. He quickly got ready, taking a bottle of water, his cell phone, and a trail map. He grabbed a granola bar for a quick breakfast and got dressed. Seeing the snow, he made sure he had boots, gloves, and a hat with his usual heavy jacket.

As he arrived at the forest, he decided to take his usual hike along the Blue Trail. This would lead him through the pine forest, past the creek, up to Lookout Point, and back down around to where the trail started. Overall, the hike would be around seven miles. James could not wait to get under way. As he entered the pine forest portion of the hike, he was amazed that there was not another person anywhere in the forest. While he enjoyed the silence, it was noticeably eerie. Amongst the conifers was a variety of bird life including black-capped chickadees and dark-eyed juncos. The thickness of the branches prevented James from seeing the sky!

As he departed the pine forest, he noticed that the sky was filled with grey clouds and that the temperature had dropped significantly. Even though he had a heavy jacket, gloves, and a winter hat, he was still getting cold. James did not mind because he was approaching his favorite place on the hike: the creek. One of James's hobbies was to observe the animal tracks near the creek. He often photographed them and looked them up upon his return home to study the animal life that was near his home. The snowfall near the frozen creek made it easy to see the prints. He noticed common ones such as squirrel and deer, but he saw one he did not recognize. He thought the print could belong to a red fox, but was not one hundred percent sure. Unfortunately, he had forgotten his camera. Instead James used the camera on his cell phone. Although the picture came out crystal clear, the camera drained the phone's battery. "Stupid battery," muttered James to himself.

As he hiked on, slightly annoyed at the phone's inefficiency, he began the hike up to Lookout Point. Near the top, the snowfall covered a root that jutted into the trail. Unbeknownst to James, he was hiking straight towards it. Before he noticed, he was on the ground with a throbbing pain in his ankle. He could immediately feel the swelling begin. Even though it was early in the day, James knew he would need to get home before the snow started again. As he got to his feet, he figured he could limp home and then call a doctor. He also knew that he could not linger and enjoy Michelle's favorite sight.

By the time James started to descend the mountain, his ankle was extremely painful and he could no longer put any weight on it. He knew he would have to call somebody. As he reached into his pocket to retrieve his cell phone, he recalled the low battery. When he pressed the power button, nothing happened. As angry thoughts about the cell phone manufacturer filled his mind, he noticed that the temperature was really starting to drop.

With the phone rendered useless, James knew he had to rest his ankle. Unfortunately, he also knew his rest had to be a short one because of the threat of snow. James honestly did not know what to do. As James stood up to try and trek on, he heard a voice in the distance. He kept hearing, "Hey, doofus, wait up. Hey!" He recognized it at once. It was Michelle.

"I thought you were at your mom's?" James questioned.

"Do you ever check your phone? I called three times saying I left early this morning and asked you to wait for me at Lookout Point! By the way, did you see somebody tripped by the creek? People really need to be careful in this weather," commented Michelle.

As James started to explain, he decided to simply tell Michelle about his ankle. Even though she was concerned about James, she could not help herself from laughing. After she composed herself, she allowed James to lean on her shoulder as he hobbled back to his house. Once at his house, they watched the snow begin to fall again from James's living room couch.

1. Which of the following best describes the setting of the passage?
   A. Modern times in a suburban area
   B. The past in a rural area
   C. The past in a metropolitan area
   D. Modern times in a rural area

2. James can be described as a character with which of the following personality traits?
   A. Stubborn and arrogant
   B. Understanding, but quick to get annoyed
   C. Angry and quick to make decisions
   D. Intelligent but selfish

3. The passage shows which of the following conflicts?

    I. Man vs. Nature

    II. Man vs. Self

    III. Man vs. Society

    IV. Man vs. Other

  A. I. and IV.

  B. II. and III.

  C. I., II., and IV.

  D. I. and II.

4. The main problem that occurred in this passage was that

  A. Michelle could not join James on a hike.

  B. James's cell phone battery died.

  C. James tripped over a root and injured his ankle.

  D. James got lost and it started snowing.

5. The personality of Michelle can best be described as

  A. forgetful.

  B. compassionate.

  C. fun loving.

  D. irresponsible.

6. Would you consider James to be a responsible hiker? What actions could he have taken to make sure he did not get caught in that difficult situation?

_____

_____

_____

_____

_____

_____

_____

_____

_____

_____

_____

_____

_____

_____

_____

_____

_____

_____

_____

_____

Exercise 10 Answers:

1. Before looking at the answer choices, look for clues found in the story itself. Based on the fact that James had a cell phone, choices B and C can immediately be eliminated. Looking at the location of the story, one can tell that there are not many people or houses around. Because of this, the answer is D.

2. Looking at the adjectives, it is important to be careful and not answer the question too fast. Choice A says that James is stubborn. There are a few points in the story in which James can be seen as stubborn such as when he goes hiking without Michelle; however, at no point of the story does he appear to be arrogant. Choice B is correct because James is understanding when Michelle says she cannot go hiking. He is also quick to get annoyed as his cell phone stops working. Choice C can be ruled out because James is not angry, and he may not even be considered quick to make decisions depending on how you look at his actions. Choice D is incorrect because at no point in the story is James selfish.

3. The correct answer to this question is D. It is correct because James has to battle nature as he faces a difficult trek back to his house through the snow and difficult terrain. He also has to battle himself to overcome the pain he is experiencing from his injured ankle.

4. All of the choices in this question involve problems James experienced except D. While two letters explain minor problems experienced, C is the main problem that occurs in the story because this situation injured him and could have presented a life-threatening dilemma.

5. Choices A and D can immediately be eliminated. While one may think that Michelle may be compassionate because she helps James back to his house, there is a better choice. Fun loving (C) is the best choice because not only does she love hiking, but she also playfully laughs at James when she finds out he was the one who tripped.

6. Even though James is a knowledgeable hiker, I do not think he is a responsible hiker. (*Restatement/Main Idea*) As the passage points out, James knows the area and trails very well. (*Information from passage*) Even though this may be true, he performed a few actions that may have turned extremely dangerous if the story did not end as it did. (*Support*) First, James went hiking alone. Even though Michelle cancelled, James should have gone with someone else or waited until she was able to go. Hiking alone can be dangerous because no

one can help you if you get hurt, as was seen in James's case until Michelle unexpectedly arrived. (*Question 2 Explanation*) Also, James did not check to see whether his cell phone worked or what the weather was going to be like that day. Any hiker should check his or her equipment before leaving, especially when traveling alone. A hiker should also know what the weather will be like the day of the hike. Weather conditions such as snow, rain, wind, or lightning can all be dangerous when hiking in the woods. (*Question 2 Explanation Continued*) Just because someone is knowledgeable about the hiking area does not mean he or she is responsible. Taking precautions to avoid danger is a characteristic of a responsible hiker. (*Conclusion*)

Drawing Conclusions

Using the information presented in a reading passage to formulate your own ideas and draw conclusions can be difficult at times. This skill often involves a slightly higher level of thinking than plot type questions. You need to take information from the selection, combine it with what you already know, and then answer the questions.

This type of questioning may include the following phrases: form an opinion, make a judgment, or make a prediction.

For some of these questions, you may need to use information from the text to form an opinion that the character may come to himself or herself. When this happens, make sure that you take into consideration all the actions the character made throughout the story. From there, think what choice would best summarize the character.

Questions asking you to make a judgment usually cause you to think about whether or not a character's course of action was the best thing to do. To answer this, first think about what you would have done in the situation and then evaluate that with how successful the character's actions were during the story. Analyzing both of those bits of information will allow you to make an informed answer effectively passing a judgment onto the character's actions.

Prediction type questions again call for you to use information given throughout the selection. This time, information will need to be used to see what action will follow or how a character may act in an upcoming situation. While the story will not give you a specific answer to this type of question, clues will be interjected throughout to help you formulate an answer.

Exercise 11:　Drawing Conclusions

To help you learn the pace at which you work, write down the time you started working on this section as well as the time you finished.

Start Time: _____

Finish Time: _____

Total Minutes: _____

Remember, when answering these questions, take what you already know into consideration with what the passage tells you. Combine the two and create an answer.

Directions:　As you read the following passage, complete the activities included.

COACH'S CAPTAIN

Kara was always interested in winning a championship for her recreation basketball team. Her team selected her as the captain for the second year in a row. Every day, she practiced dribbling skills and foul shots, and ran "suicides" in her driveway. Her friends would say that Kara lived for the game of basketball.

As Kara arrived at practice, her dad wished her luck and told her he would be back at 8:30 to pick her up. As she stepped out of the car, Kara realized that some kid was standing outside the gym doors. He looked utterly a mess. His shoelaces were untied and his shoes looked like the only thing holding them together was the mud that was caked on them. The way he tried to kick the empty soda can told Kara that this kid did not have an athletic bone in his body.

Kara ran into the gym excited to start practice. As she entered, the strange kid seemed to follow. Coach said, "Kara, great to see you! As captain, I would like to introduce you to the newest member of our team. This is Marcus. Can you practice with him today?"

1. Using the passage, formulate an opinion Kara would have about Marcus.

_____

_____

_____

_____

_____

_____

_____

Immediately, Kara's mood went from being excited about the upcoming season to having a sense of dread. She saw her team's hope of a championship fading fast as well. She knew that the coach would be unhappy if she said "No" to showing Marcus around, but she needed to practice with the team, not serve as a babysitter. "Okay, Coach," she muttered softly. "Let's go, Marcus," she commanded. Marcus was excited to follow her—in fact a little too excited. As he raced after Kara, his shoelaces got tangled, causing him to trip. This wipeout in the middle of the gymnasium did not seem to faze Marcus, but Kara was even more embarrassed and disgusted at her new role. The season was already going down the tubes minutes into the first practice. How could Kara not leave Marcus unattended, but still get some practice time on the court?

Almost instantaneously, Kara had an idea. She saw her friend Russell dribbling in the corner of the gym. While Russell was a decent player on defense, he did not receive much playing time. Russell also was one of the nicest kids on the team. Even though Coach told Kara to help Marcus out, she did not see anything wrong with introducing him to Russell. That is exactly what she did.

2. Using the first and second passages, make a judgment about Kara's actions. Was she correct in leaving Marcus with Russell?

_____

_____

_____

_____

_____

_____

3. Before reading on, make a prediction about what will happen with Russell and Marcus in the gymnasium? In your prediction, include information about what Kara will be doing.

_____

_____

_____

_____

_____

_____

Russell and Marcus spent time together at practice. Russell began to practice free throws and Marcus eagerly rebounded all the shots passing them back to Russell at the foul line. They were really enjoying themselves. As Kara observed this, she snuck out onto the court to practice some defensive drills. As usual, she was at the top of her game. She felt great having set up the new kid with the not-so-good kid as well. Just as she was thinking this, she made an extraordinary steal of a pass, raced down the court, and scored a lay-up. Her teammates were quite impressed as was her coach. Unfortunately, this joviality was short lived. "Kara, get over here!" yelled the coach. "I thought I told you to keep an eye on Marcus! What type of captain do you think you are? There is more to being a leader than scoring points for your team. You're done for today."

She was stunned. She did not see herself as a leader on the team, just a talented player. Kara thought what she had done was fine; nobody got hurt and she got to practice. She thought the situation was a win-win for everyone.

4. After reading this section, in your opinion, did the coach react correctly?

_____

_____

_____

_____

_____

_____

5. Predict why you think the coach was so upset with Kara's actions.

_____

_____

_____

_____

_____

_____

_____

When Kara was waiting on the bench for practice to end, she was quite perplexed. Coach had never gotten remotely angry at her and always seemed to be very proud of all of her efforts on and off the court. As Kara was pondering what exactly was happening, her coach sat next to her. "Kara, can I talk to you?" he asked in a fatherly way. She nodded with her eyes on the floor. "The reason I asked you to look after Marcus was because he is my son! He is not old enough to play on the team but always wants to come to practice." Immediately Kara recognized Marcus from being in the stands with the coach's wife last year. She was left feeling extremely stupid at this moment.

Coach went on to explain that he felt confident in trusting Kara to look after his son because he knew that she was practicing so much at home. He also told her that the rest of the team needed some work to be ready for the season to start. Kara apologized for acting the way she did and for disappointing her coach. The coach was not angry at his star player for long, especially when he saw how upset she was. Just as the conversation was wrapping up, practice ended. Kara said good-bye to Marcus and his dad and eagerly ran to her parents' car excited to return tomorrow for another day of practice.

6. Why should the coach not be angry at Kara? Also, what does this story tell about Kara's abilities as a captain? Would you consider Kara a good captain? Explain.

_____

_____

_____

_____

_____

_____

_____

_____

_____

_____

_____

_____

_____

_____

_____

_____

_____

_____

_____

Exercise 11 Answers:

1. Looking at what we know about Kara, we can tell that she is extremely competitive and that sports are important to her. Marcus, on the other hand, "does not have an athletic bone in his body." As a result, it is to be concluded that Kara will see Marcus as a pain or someone that will get in the way of her goal. Her opinion of Marcus is probably that he is a burden, a dork, or someone who will just be useless to the team.

2. There are two possible responses to this question. The first answer would be that Kara's actions were correct. This answer can be supported by the information that Kara did not leave Marcus unattended. She left him in the care of one of the nicest players on the team. Also, when she left, she noticed how much fun both boys were having.

   The second answer would be that Kara did not make the correct decision. This answer can be supported by the fact that Kara had not followed the coach's directions. The coach specifically gave her the responsibility to care for Marcus and that is what she should have done.

3. This type of question can have a variety of answers. Two possible responses are given. One response would be that Marcus and Russell continue to have a good time. Kara may go back later to thank Russell, and then pay attention to Marcus for the last few minutes of practice. Another response might be that Marcus might get hurt while in the care of Russell or that the coach would notice that Kara was not where she was supposed to be. Any of these choices can be supported by your personal experiences that may back up your answer.

4. The most logical way to respond to this question would be to say that the coach was right in reacting the way he did. From your own experience you might discuss that coaches are like teachers, and both are figures of authority. These people usually command respect from players. Therefore, a player should follow the directions of a coach. When he or she does not, it can be seen as disrespectful or damaging to the team.

   However, you may also respond by paying attention to the fact that Kara was a star player. Usually a coach is a little more understanding of the wishes of his or her star. Kara always seemed to practice hard and have the best interests of the team in mind. Therefore, you can also argue that the coach overreacted.

5. This prediction also can have a variety of responses. You may say that the coach felt disrespected, was having a bad practice, or was concerned about one of his new players. Any of those responses would be considered correct.

6. Kara's coach should not have been angry at Kara. (*Restatement of Question 1*) Kara did the exact same thing that he himself did with his son. (*Support*) It was the coach's responsibility to watch his son. He should not have left it up to one of his players. All Kara did was find someone else to watch Marcus. (*Explanation*)

   Kara, though, was a good team captain. (*Answer to questions 2 and 3*) The fact that Russell agreed to watch Marcus showed her abilities as a captain. (*Support from story*) A captain needs to have the respect of the team and a leadership role. Kara clearly had that because Russell agreed without objection. (*Explanation*) Another reason Kara makes a good captain is because of her dedication to her sport. (*Support from story*) Just because she is not at an official practice does not mean she is not thinking about her team. She dedicates what seems like hours practicing to improve her own skills. (*Explanation*) Finally, Kara accepts the coach's decision to bench her after she did not listen to his instructions. (*Support*) She did not throw a tantrum or argue on the court. She waited to hear his explanation and, after listening, put the incident behind her. (*Analysis of story and explanation*) All of these qualities make Kara an effective team captain. (*Conclusion*)

Exercise 12: Drawing Conclusions

To help you learn the pace at which you work, write down the time you started working on this section as well as the time you finished.

Start Time: _____

Finish Time: _____

Total Minutes: _____

Directions: Use the following passage to answer the questions that follow.

HOME ON THE RANGE

As Conrad woke up, he knew that it was going to be a long day. Not only did the first day of school usually bring about a sense of dread, but he also had a lot of chores to do before even thinking about getting ready. Life on the farm was not easy. Conrad knew that he had to check the chicken house to see if any eggs were laid, check to see if the goats had water, and open the gate so the cows could enter the pasture.

As he got out of bed, he noticed that the clock said 5:00 A.M. He sighed because he knew it would be a long week. Getting back into the habit of doing chores, catching the bus, attending school, coming home to help out on the farm, and finally doing homework was not exactly easy. He remembered how last year went. His teacher, Ms. Sharplert, kept sending home notes saying, "Conrad does not pay attention in class. He always seems to be fading out, and rarely has his homework completed." She, being from the city and all, just did not get his life.

Throughout these ponderings, Conrad already filled up a basket with eggs, checked on the goats, and let the cows out. Now, he definitely needed to remember to go and take a shower. Thinking back to last year brought back another not so pleasant memory. "Hey Hoss, did you sleep with the cows last night?" were chants Conrad remembered as he tried to find a seat on the bus. He woke up late that day, and went straight from doing his chores to the school bus, leaving out a few other important steps to morning preparation. Today, being the first day and all, Conrad knew he better take a shower.

After rushing through breakfast, Conrad almost forgot his lunch. His mother reminded him and gave him a good-luck kiss on the check. Walking to the bus stop, he forcefully tried to rub the lipstick off his cheek. You could not start seventh grade with your mother's lipstick on you face, that's for sure.

With the first two disasters of the day avoided, Conrad trudged through the fields on his way to Grey Street. Even though it was early, the street was dusty from the summer heat. The bottoms of his jeans were dusty, but Conrad thought to himself, "At least I showered." He found a spot on the empty bench and began to observe the area waking up. The farms were coming to life as the dreary animals began to wander into the fields and their owners began the maintenance of their land. Awakening Conrad from his daydream was the yellow school bus meandering down the winding road. He knew that finding a seat would not be a problem because his was the first stop. Most of the other students lived much closer to the school. Conrad knew he had at least a half an hour before arriving at school so he decided to get some sleep.

"Okay, everyone off. Make sure you don't leave anything on this bus!" barked the bus driver, startling Conrad awake. He groggily departed the bus trying to rub the sleepiness out of his eyes.

"Farmer Conrad, you forgot your lunch. Here," said one of the kids getting off the bus after Conrad. It was way too early in the year for the mocking to begin. Conrad walked through the halls, entered his classroom, and hung up his backpack. Having been up for three hours already, he was finally waking up. He figured the teacher would be here in a few minutes, and then the real fun of the day would start.

"Howdy, class! Take out a piece of paper and a pen. We are going to have a writing assignment," Mr. Grafos excitedly instructed. Immediately, Conrad thought that this guy sounded exactly like his Dad. That thought was quickly replaced with the fact that a writing assignment needed to be completed. Last year Conrad remembered Ms. Sharplert giving an assignment to write about anything you wanted. The only thing going through Conrad's mind was those trained circus bears that ride the unicycle. After reading the essay, she recommended that he go talk to the guidance counselor.

Mr. Grafos began to write the assignment on the board amidst whispers of "Can I borrow a pen? What is this guy thinking? It's the first day of school!" and "Ugh, I don't have any paper."

"Okay, class, today's assignment deals with an aspect of life that may be unfamiliar to you but very real to some of your neighbors. I know many of you live in town, but some of you also live on farms. I, myself, grew up on a farm. I want you to partner up with someone who lives in an area of town different from you. Talk. Discuss what your chores, responsibilities, and everyday life is like. Then, write a compare/contrast essay about your two lifestyles."

Conrad felt like his luck in school was about to change and that this might be a great year after all.

1. Why might Ms. Sharplert be wrong in assuming that Conrad does not pay attention because he is not interested in school?

   A. Conrad looked like he was daydreaming.

   B. Students in the city she grew up in paid close attention to the teacher.

   C. By the time Conrad was in class, he was already awake for close to four hours.

   D. Conrad felt school was an unpleasant place to be.

2. What conclusion can be made from the third paragraph about Conrad's relationship with other students?

   A. The lifestyle Conrad lives often caused him to be misunderstood by his peers.

   B. The reason why students do not like him is because Conrad is unclean.

   C. Conrad is irresponsible and other people cannot rely on him.

   D. Conrad is a loner and chooses to seclude himself from the other kids on the bus.

3. Looking at Conrad's preparation before school, what opinion does he have of himself?

   A. Conrad takes special consideration to prepare for the day because he is proud of how he looks.

   B. Conrad is not interested at all in his appearance.

   C. Conrad expects the worst to happen, but he tries to carefully prepare for the day to prevent previous mistakes from happening again.

   D. Conrad tries to show everyone else just how good he is by carefully selecting the clothes he will wear to school.

4. All of the following show that Conrad and the class have the same opinion of the writing assignment EXCEPT

    A. whispers of "Ugh, I don't have a pen."

    B. Conrad's memory of a writing assignment that Ms. Sharplert assigned last year.

    C. whispers of "What is this guy thinking? It's the first day of school!"

    D. a student asking to borrow a pen.

5. What bit of information causes Conrad to predict that this will be a better school year than last year?

    A. Conrad thinking that Mr. Grafos sounded like his father

    B. The student on the bus returning Conrad's lunch

    C. Mr. Grafos growing up on a farm

    D. Mr. Grafos's assignment to get to know a peer in the classroom

6. Evaluate Mr. Grafos's assignment. Was this a good learning opportunity for his class? What was he hoping his students would learn from each other?

_____

_____

_____

_____

_____

_____

_____

_____

_____

_____

Exercise 12 Answers:

1. C. Conrad had a variety of chores to do before going to school. As mentioned in the second paragraph, Conrad wakes up very early for a child his age. Also, a reason why he may not complete his homework could be his farm responsibilities. Helping out his family may take away from the time he has to focus on schoolwork.

2. A. The story mentions that Conrad is the only child to board the bus at his bus stop. Most of the students of the school live in town. Because of this, Conrad and his peers live seemingly in two different worlds causing them not to relate well to each other.

3. C. Conrad does not seem to think too highly of himself, so it is safe to say that he does not take the time to get ready to impress anyone. Having had some embarrassing moments at school, Conrad takes careful preparation to prevent them from happening again.

4. D. Choices A, B, and C all show that the students are not looking forward to the writing assignment. However, asking to borrow a pen does not have anything to do with the class not wanting to write.

5. C. Unlike last year, Conrad thinks that he and the teacher may have a better chance of understanding each other because the teacher grew up on a farm as well.

6. Mr. Grafos's assignment may not be popular amongst the students, but it is a good assignment. (*Restatement of the question*) This assignment will cause people to talk to people they may never talk to otherwise. (*Support from analysis of passage*) Not only will they have to talk to each other, but there are terrific learning opportunities for all the students of the class. (*Support from analysis of passage*) While this may not be seen as book learning, it will offer a chance to learn life skills. (*Support from analysis of passage*) Students will have to actually talk to each other and think. (*Support from analysis of passage*) This is not a question that can be answered in one sentence or by one member of the group. (*Support from analysis of passage*) Mr. Grafos is hoping that students will see what they have in common with their peers along with what makes them different. (*Support from analysis of passage*) He may have experienced problems growing up as a farm child himself, and may be trying to provide a more tolerant classroom for all students. (*Support from analysis of passage*) Mr. Grafos's assignment is forcing students to think outside their comfort zones and write about their experiences. (*Support from analysis of passage*) Even though this requires work that students do not like, it is an extremely valuable learning experience for them. (*Conclusion*)

Chapter 3
Writing

The NJ ASK6 requires you to respond to two types of writing prompts: persuasive and explanatory. Writing a full essay in a specific amount of time can be stressful if you do not know what to expect. This chapter will define both prompts and provide examples and helpful hints for successfully completing each. Also included is a series of practice exercises for you to complete.

Here are some helpful tips for the writing section of the test:

Know your time! The time you have to answer each prompt is different. For the persuasive prompt, 45 minutes will be given. For the explanatory prompt, you'll get 25 minutes to complete the task. No matter which prompt you are doing, you should allow yourself time to prewrite, write, and proofread your work.

As with the reading questions, **take time to carefully read over what the prompt is asking you to do.** You will not receive credit if your essay does not relate to the question, so make sure you understand what your task is. Read the directions over two or three times just to make sure you get started on the right path.

Focus on content. The rubric for the NJ ASK6 focuses mainly on the content you include in your writing. If you get stuck on the spelling of a word, do the best you can! Try to get it as close as possible, but don't spend too much time on it. Spend more time providing support, examples, and details for your essay.

Check your answers. Just because you place the last period at the end of your last sentence does not mean you are finished. Go through your essay to make sure all your sentences make sense. Also, make sure your essay stays on task and does not drift onto other topics. Remember what the prompt is asking you. Also, be sure to add more details wherever you feel your message is unclear or not fully developed.

Do not work past the stop sign on the bottom right corner of your test booklet! If you do, your test will be voided and will not count. So, pay attention to the directions and your test booklets to avoid any possible complications.

EXPLANATORY PROMPTS

Explanatory prompts ask you to respond to a specific topic or quote. The test will give you a topic or quotation that you will need to explain by discussing personal experiences or examples. As with any other writing assignment, you should follow the process of prewriting, writing, and revising. However, with this assignment, you may have to work faster than you are used to working. Don't let the time factor take away from the overall quality of your writing.

In this chapter, the practice exercises will take you through the steps of the writing process. Advice and hints accompany each one. The first in the series of exercises will be a model for you to follow. It will go through each of the steps in the process for the same prompt. That way, you will be able to see how the essay developed into a finished product.

Prewriting

The first thing you need to do after reading the prompt is to organize your thoughts. When you have only 25 minutes to write, time is precious. Because time is precious, you need to organize your thoughts so you have a clear focus and do not waste a single minute. Using the following strategies will allow you to do this.

First, if the prompt is asking you to explain a quote, rewrite the quote in your own words. This will make sure you understand what the quote means. After you understand what the quote means, then start a list of examples of what the quotation means to your life or examples that show its meaning. If you do not agree with the quote or do not feel it applies to your life, do not write that. Basically, the prompt is telling you that the quote applies to your life. Do not fight the prompt. Even if you do not agree that the quote applies to your life, do the best you can to try and link it even if everything you are writing is not entirely relevant to you. Above all, be consistent!

If your prompt asks you to write about a time that you experienced something, you will need to provide specific examples. For prewriting, list 3 or 4 times in your life in which you have experienced what the prompt is talking about. In your essay, you may not be able to describe all of them, so select the one or two you feel you will be able to best develop.

Example 1:

Consider how the following quotation is related to you.

> "All men desire knowledge."
> —Aristotle (384 BC–322 BC)

Write an essay explaining what this quotation means to you. Be sure to use specific details and examples.

My Prewriting

Quote in my own words: People want to always learn new things.

Examples:

1. *Desire to go to the moon in the 1960s*

2. *Study the animals and plants in the Amazon*

3. *My desire to go to college*

4. *When I read a how-to book about making a website*

Example 2:

Goals are an important part of life. Think about a time in your life when you set a goal for yourself and achieved it.

Write an essay about how you felt going through the process and how you felt when you finally achieved your goal. Explain whether the process of working towards the goal or the achievement of the goal itself was more rewarding. Use examples and details to support your answer.

My Prewriting

1. *Trying to make the middle-school baseball team*

2. *Trying to get on the Honor Roll*

3. *Working on getting an autograph from all the living baseball Hall of Famers*

4. *Doing chores to save money to buy a new video game*

After looking at the list, I can write the most about the last two, but I will select the third.

Exercise 1: Prewriting

For this exercise, you will complete the prewriting component for 5 prompts. Time yourself. Limit the time you spend on each prompt to 3 or 4 minutes.

1. As part of a writing class, you have been asked to show how the following quotation is related to your life.

   "It is our choices . . . that show who we truly are, far more than our abilities."

   —J. K. Rowling

   Write an essay using details and examples telling what the quotation means to you.

_____

_____

_____

_____

_____

_____

_____

_____

_____
---

2. Consider how the following quotation is related to you.

   "What is defeat? Nothing but education;
   nothing but the first step to something better."

   —Wendell Phillips (1811–84)

Write an essay explaining what the quote means by using examples from your life as well as any other details that may apply.

_____

_____

_____

_____

_____

_____

_____

3. Responsibility can come in many different forms. Use details and examples from your life or the life of someone you know to explain the following quote:

> "We are made wise not by the recollection of our past,
> but by responsibility for our future."

> —George Bernard Shaw

Write an essay that explains how this quote relates to responsibility.

_____

_____

_____

_____

_____

_____

_____

4. Strength can be found in some surprising places. Identify a time in your life when you found a source of personal strength.

Write an essay using details and examples of how this moment of strength has had a positive impact on your life.

_____

_____

_____

_____

_____

_____

_____

5. One of the hardest things to do is work with someone who has completely different ideas or views from yours. However, in the end, having tolerance for others can provide a valuable learning experience.

Think of a time when you worked with someone very different from yourself, and write an essay explaining what that experience was like as well as what you learned.

_____

_____

_____

_____

_____

_____

_____

Exercise 1 Answers:

With essay responses, there is no one correct answer. All of the answers to these prompts depend mainly on your experiences in life. With that being said, the answers provided can be used as a guide if you cannot think of anything to write.

1. With this quote, it will be important for the writer to explain how choices are more important than ability alone. Examples may include an athlete who has all the talent in the world but never practices. That athlete may never make a difference on any team he or she is on. Another example may be a comparison of a person who is naturally funny. Examples may include whether that person uses humor for making fun of people or to cheer people up. That choice will show what type a person he or she is much more than just saying that person is funny.

2. For this quotation, you should think about a time in life when you may have lost or did not succeed in something. Instead of giving up, are there any incidences that motivated you to try harder or be better? Common situations that you can write about are putting more effort into studies after failing a test, or practicing more after not making a team or not winning a championship.

3. The final quote is the most challenging. You may need to think of lessons in history or events in the news. Or you can think of your own experiences with leaders and/or responsibility in general. An example to explain this quote would be to discuss people who only talk about what they did in the past and never plan on doing anything in the present or future. Just because they may have been great in the past does not mean they will continue to be great. So, how you plan for the future will truly make you intelligent, not just how you remember the past.

4. While this is not a quote, you will still need to provide specific examples that apply to your life. Some ideas to consider are a time when you or someone you know has stood up to a bully, or defended someone. Another idea may be to even discuss a time when you knew telling the truth would get you into trouble, but you did so anyway.

5. This final example is similar to the expression "Don't judge a book by its cover." Examples you may wish to write about include: having a teacher that you may have hated at the beginning of the school year, but then he became one of your favorites; not wanting to work with a certain person on a group project but then becoming friends with her; or not liking a new student until you actually got to know the person.

Writing

After spending 2 to 3 minutes on your prewriting, you should spend about
20 minutes on the actual writing of your answer. When writing your essay, follow
normal essay format.

Start your essay with an introduction. In your introduction, try to start with an
attention-grabbing opener. You can work the quote into your first sentence or
possibly ask a question. Following the attention-grabber, restate the purpose of the
prompt. Finally, you may wish to introduce your examples.

The body of your essay should contain about 2 paragraphs. You may wish
to include 2 examples to support the quote, one per body paragraph. Start the
paragraph off by stating the example. Then, explain how the example is related to
the prompt. Be sure to explain how the example is related to you if the prompt asks
that. A final sentence should sum up the first body paragraph as well.

The second body paragraph should present the second example. After
introducing the example, follow the same format for the first body paragraph. If
you have more examples, add them. If adding more examples, be sure you leave
yourself enough time to write an effective conclusion.

When you get to the conclusion, your goal is to sum up your paper without repeating
the exact same words. While this should be similar to your introduction, it should not be
identical. You might want to restate the main idea of your passage and to sum up your
examples. End strongly, and let the reader know exactly how your examples relate to
the prompt.

Example 1:

Consider how the following quotation is related to you.

"All men desire knowledge."
—Aristotle (384 BC–322 BC)

Write an essay explaining what this quotation means to you. Be sure to use specific details and examples.

Have you ever looked at an event or watched something on television and wondered why or how that happened? As Aristotle said, "All men desire knowledge." People are always curious about new things and wanting to expand what they already know to new levels. Examples of this can be seen throughout history as well as in my own life.

History is a terrific example of how people are always trying to go to new areas of knowledge. One example of this can be seen with the space program of the 1960s. Space was seen as the "final frontier" and considered the last unknown location. The quest for knowledge fueled countries such as the United States and Soviet Union in the development of programs to actually see what was out there. It also created a competition to see who could get there first. Through this desire for knowledge, information was gathered about the moon, planets, and solar system. Also, technology was developed as a result of the space program that still impacts our lives today.

A similar, more modern exploration for knowledge is occurring in the rain forests today. Scientists are trying to learn about plants and animals before they disappear. To the amazement of the science world, a variety of new animals and plant life is still being discovered and creatures once thought to be extinct are being rediscovered. The main desire of knowledge in this area is to possibly find cures for diseases of today. While these cures are currently being studied, one positive result of this quest for knowledge is that this desire is leading to rain forests being protected.

While those are worldwide "desires for knowledge," I feel that I have this quest within myself. Even though I am in sixth grade, I hope to one day go to college. By going to college, I will expand what I know about topics. Also, I may take a variety of art, science, and history classes that I would never take in middle school or high school. By going deeper into these subjects, I will be able to understand the world around me on a different level. By learning about history, I will be much more knowledgeable about the world today.

Finally, I am interested in computers. I use computers for homework, to talk to my friends, and to play games. Reading about how the computer works helps me in all of these areas. Last year this new game came out for the computer. My friends all got the game and were much better than me. I did not always enjoy losing, so I began to research how to do better. By reading a how-to book, it explained certain tricks and clues about how I could play the game better. I read that book in two days! I was much happier when I had the knowledge to be at the same level as my friends.

People's desire to learn more has been a very important part of history and of my life. Many discoveries were made because of this desire. Hopefully, humans will always have this want to learn more, because with that want, he or she can make the world a much better place.

Example 2:

Goals are an important part of life. Think about a time in your life when you set a goal for yourself and achieved it.

Write an essay about how you felt going through the process and how you felt when you finally achieved the goal you had set for yourself. Explain whether the process of working towards the goal or the achievement of the goal itself was more rewarding. Use examples and details to support your answer.

Goals are an important part of all people's lives. They usually allow people to better themselves or their surroundings in some way. While many people consider accomplishing the goal the most important part, sometimes the process that brings them to that part is more fun and worthwhile. It is like the phrase, "the thrill of the hunt." Many people find the actions and events leading up to the goal much more exciting, and I would have to agree.

A few years ago, I started to collect autographs of the players in the Baseball Hall of Fame who are still alive. This goal started with some research. First, I got a list of all the Hall of Famers in age order. The older players were usually easier to get than some of the younger ones. Next came some more research. I began to write letters to some of the players to see who would sign through the mail. Some players wrote back and said to just send the baseball to be signed, some said how much they charge, some said no, and I never heard back from some. Next came some more research. Over the years some autograph shows were held within a few hours of where I live. I would check the lists to see who the players were and to see how many chores I would need to do to be able to afford it.

I needed to have my Dad, grandfather, and sometimes even my Mom drive me to these shows. That was the best part about trying to achieve this goal, the time and talks I had with my family going to these shows. Many of the autographs I could not afford became Christmas or birthday gifts. Those became the prized parts of my collection. Another part of the process that I began to enjoy more than anything was sharing the stories of my new autographs with my parents. This is how the process definitely became more rewarding than the goal.

While new Hall of Famers get added every year, this goal will keep expanding. And that is a good thing because the challenge will allow me to continue to spend time with my family and add more stories to the collection.

Exercise 2 Writing:

For each of the following five sample exercises, limit yourself to 20 minutes of writing. You should get into the habit of managing your time, and trying to write for the full amount of time. What you can accomplish in that time will be an accurate indicator of what you will be able to do on test day. Look back at your prewriting. Remember, your prewriting will not be graded, so if your ideas are not working out, change them!

1. As part of a writing class, you have been asked to show how the following quotation is related to your life.

> "It is our choices . . . that show who we truly are,
> far more than our abilities."
>
> —J. K. Rowling

Write an essay using details and examples telling what the quotation means to you.

_____

_____

_____

_____

_____

_____

_____

_____

_____

_____

_____

_____

2. Consider how the following quotation relates to your experiences.

"What is defeat? Nothing but education;
nothing but the first step to something better."

—Wendell Phillips (1811–84)

Write an essay explaining what the quote means by using examples from your life as well as any other details that may apply.

_____

_____

_____

_____

_____

_____

_____

_____

_____

_____

_____

_____

_____

3. Responsibility can come in many different forms. Use details and examples from your life or the knowledge you have to explain the following quote.

"We are made wise not by the recollection of our past, but by responsibility for our future."

—George Bernard Shaw

Write an essay that explains how this quote relates to responsibility.

_____

_____

_____

_____

_____

_____

_____

_____

_____

_____

_____

_____

_____

4. Strength can be found in some surprising places. Identify a time in your life when you found a source of personal strength.

Write an essay using details and examples of how this moment of strength has had a positive impact on your life.

_____

_____

_____

_____

_____

_____

_____

_____

_____

_____

_____

_____

_____

_____

5. One of the hardest things to do is work with someone who has completely different ideas or views from yours. However, having tolerance for others can provide a valuable learning experience.

Think of a time when you worked with someone very different from yourself. Now write an essay explaining what that experience was like as well as what you learned.

_____

_____

_____

_____

_____

_____

_____

_____

_____

_____

_____

_____

_____

_____

_____

Exercise 2 Answers:

Remember, there are no specific right or wrong answers to these prompts. The following sample responses are to be used only as guidelines to compare with your own writing.

1. *People have many different abilities that set them apart from each other. Abilities do not tell as much about people as the choices they make about using those abilities. Many times people let their talents go to waste or use them in a way that does not benefit anyone. That tells a lot about them. It can tell just as much about people if they work hard at using their talent to better themselves or the people around them.*

An example of this is how people can use their ability to make others laugh. If a person uses humor to make fun of people or to put others down, then that choice shows that person is not a nice person or even be a bully. However, if that person uses a joke to cheer someone up who is in a bad mood, that choice shows the person is a good friend. I have a friend who always tries to make a joke at our lunch table when someone is not that happy. He is always trying to cheer us up and it usually works. Here, his talent is definitely not wasted and his choice to use it shows everyone at the table what a good friend he is.

Another example of how choices tell more than ability can be seen in my classroom. There is one student who does pretty well on all of his tests, but always ends up getting 80s in the class because he does not do his homework. He is very smart and can always answer questions, but he is lazy. A friend of mine studies every night, goes in for extra help, and always does her homework. She gets the same grade as the other kid. But, when it comes to working with a partner or in a group, I will always try and get in the group with my friend. The reason is not because she is my friend, but because of the choices she makes. She may not be as smart as the lazy kid, but she chooses to work hard and make the most of every class. She is an example of a good student who uses as much of the ability that she has to do as best as she can.

Ability is terrific to have. But if you don't use it, that talent is a waste. Anyone can be naturally talented, but the choices people make about what to do with that ability truly shows their character and who they are.

2. *Defeat can be an extremely difficult feeling to accept. Wendell Phillips once said that defeat is "Nothing but education; nothing but the first step to something better." At the time you lose you might not feel like anything good*

can come from it, but valuable lessons can happen. A loss may cause you to try harder. By having the motivation to try harder, you can improve your skills or chances of success.

An example of this can be seen in my math class. We started to work on geometry problems, and I thought I knew exactly what I was doing on the homework. It seemed very easy in class, and I was able to finish the worksheet without even bringing it home. The next day in class was a different story. When the teacher started to go over the homework, I realized that I got every problem wrong. I felt like a complete idiot. I was also very nervous because we were having a test at the end of the next week. I went home and asked my mom for help. She suggested that I go in the next morning for extra help. I really felt like I was not smart now. Math used to be so easy! The next morning I shyly went in for help. I continued to go in that whole week. The teacher showed me that I was just making a simple, easy-to-fix error in all of the problems. She made me feel that I had a chance to be smart again and was not dumb at all. Because of her help, I did very well on the test and became a much better math student than before.

Another example that proves this quote happened at the beginning of basketball season. At a scrimmage we had before the season started, I was at the free throw line at the beginning of the fourth quarter. We were down by two points when I got fouled. I missed both shots and we ended up losing the game by five points. Even though my misses did not lose the game, I could have tied it. After that I would practice 50 shots every day after I got home from school. My dad would come out and rebound for me when he got home. We had a great time, and I became a better shooter. Even if I never had the opportunity to go to the free throw line again, I wanted to be better for myself.

Defeat is hard to accept for anyone, whether you lose the Super Bowl or fail a test. Fighting through that defeat though shows what type of person you truly are. Wendell Phillips was correct when he said defeat can actually teach valuable lessons and actually improve my life!

3. *The past is always an important part of our lives. However, we cannot live in it. Being smart means to remember the past while having a "responsibility for our future." Intelligence is learning from the mistakes of the past so they do not happen again.*

Many times people are happy about what they achieved in the past. Just because a person did something terrific two years ago does not mean anything good is happening today. I know I made Honor Roll in third grade. Even though that was a great achievement for me at that time, that does not mean I am doing well in school now. It would be my responsibility to continue to do well in school. Getting a hundred and then failing the next five tests does not mean that I am doing well in school. I can think about that hundred all I want, but I would still be failing the class.

Another example of how this quote is true is by looking at history. Just because somebody remembers a lot about the past does not mean he or she is brilliant. What that person does with the information determines how brilliant he or she is. Learning from the mistakes of the past or what was done currently in the past is what is useful. If you look at Martin Luther King's "I Have a Dream" speech, you can see that ideas were taken from many past writings and documents. Martin Luther King didn't just look at the documents and say, "See, people should have these rights." He quoted the Declaration of Independence, ideas of the Constitution, and writings of many famous Americans to show what their dream actually was for America. He saw that he had a responsibility to future generations. He did not rest on ideas of what happened in the past, he dreamt of what could be. As time goes on, King's responsibility to the future is allowing his dream to slowly be realized.

Responsibility can mean many different things to many different people. Many people feel that they need to have a responsibility to remember the past, and many people feel that they have a responsibility to improve the future. As George Bernard Shaw said in his quote, true responsibility is using the past to prepare for a better tomorrow.

4. *Strength does not always have to mean who is the biggest kid in the sixth grade or who can lift the largest amount of weights. Strength can actually mean something that does not involve being physically strong at all. Many people can find this quality at surprising times when they stand up to a bully or tell the truth in a difficult situation.*

During lunch, people usually always have to sit with people in their own grade. People usually sit with friends, but there always was this one sixth grader who sat alone. Everyday an eighth grader would go up to the kid who sat by himself and ask for money. Everyday, the poor sixth grader would give him his extra snack money. This went on for a week, and the sixth grader never told a lunch aide, a teacher, or the principal. Finally, a student who sat at my table said that somebody should help our classmate out. I was about half the size of the eighth grader; however, I went right up to the eighth grader and told him to stop asking for money. The eighth grader looked shocked. I did not do anything vicious or mean, but sounded authoritative. After I stuck up for my classmate, I just went back to eating my lunch. It was amazing that I suddenly found the strength inside myself and stuck up for someone I did not even really know. The eighth grader did stop asking for money though.

Another time that shows how a person can find strength within themselves is when I had to tell the truth about something that I had done. When I was at a friend's house, I accidentally dropped a glass when I was trying to pour myself a glass of water. My friend walked in and started laughing because I had a look of panic on my face. The same time my friend was laughing at me, his dad walked in. His dad assumed that he was laughing because he broke the glass and began to yell at him. My friend was sent to his room. He did not blame me or anything. I felt horrible as I sat on the couch. Even though I was afraid I would get yelled at, I knew I had to explain to his dad that I was the one who dropped the glass. I timidly explained what happened to his dad. I was nervous, but I did so anyway. When I was done, my friend's dad thanked me and apologized to his son. I felt much better after telling the truth and was actually proud about the strength I found in myself.

Both of these events definitely had a positive impact on my life. Just finding out that I could stand up for myself or others in a difficult time made me feel great. When I stood up for my peer and my friend, I felt like I did the right thing. Hopefully when faced with similar situations in the future, I will be able to find this strength again.

5. *Many times we look for friends that are exactly like us. When we surround ourselves with people that are the same as us, we think we will always have something to talk about and nothing to fight about. But does this make us better people? Will this make a person learn anything? Sometimes the best lessons can be learned from someone completely different from yourself.*

When I was in fourth grade, I had to switch classes for reading. During the first week of school, I thought my homeroom class was great, but I hated going to reading. The teacher was the complete opposite of me. I was shy and extremely quiet. She was loud and in your face. I would go home to my mom and say that I did not want to be in that class anymore. My mom told me that it was way too early in the year and to give her a try. About halfway through the year, I began to realize that I was doing some pretty good work in that class. Even though my grades were not super high, I was learning a lot. By the end of the school year, she became my favorite teacher. Now that I am in sixth grade, I still go back and visit her when I have the chance. I know if I ever need advice on a school related problem, I could go back to her.

My first opinion of her was extremely wrong, and I am glad my mom made me stick it out for the year!

Another example of learning from someone who is different from me occurred this year in my writing class. The teacher would always pick groups by who was sitting around you. So, when we got this one assignment, I was annoyed that this one kid in particular was in the group. He was never in school, he never did any work, and I was sure he would bring my grade down. When the teacher introduced the assignment, that kid was absent. Already this was turning into a nightmare, because now the group would either have to catch him up or do the work for him. The assignment included writing a summary, and drawing a book cover for a short story we read in class. Our group, especially me, could not draw the cover if our lives depended on it. The next day in class, the group did not expect much even though the absent student was back. Much to my surprise, though, he happened to be a terrific artist! He could not write well, but we had already finished the summary. Not only did he draw the cover, he also tried to teach us how to draw what it was. It was great. We were two completely different people. He never did any homework and did not seem to care about grades while I did. But, because of him I was able to get a very good grade and pick up some drawing tips.

These two examples show that you need to give people a chance. Sometimes they will do more than surprise you, they will help you. Like the old saying goes, "Never judge a book by its cover." People are too complicated and interesting for anyone to be able to learn everything about them just by looking at them. So the next time you see somebody different from you, you might be right that they are different, but that may turn out to be a good thing, so give them a chance to impress you.

PERSUASIVE PROMPTS

The second type of writing prompt you are asked to respond to on the NJ ASK6 is a persuasive prompt. For a persuasive prompt, the writer is required to convince the reader to agree to a certain side by presenting facts and examples.

For the persuasive prompt, you will have 45 minutes to prewrite, write, and revise your essay. Use your time wisely. Even though it is 20 more minutes than the other prompt, you will not have time to waste and should use every minute of it.

Some general tips to write your best persuasive response:

- Try to avoid using the first person and personal examples.

- It is okay to make up believable statistics to use as support.

- If you are asked to write a letter, be sure to include a greeting (Dear Mr. Michaels:). Again, it is acceptable to use a made-up name.

- Finally, choose a side! Do not provide information for both sides of the argument.

Your response to the persuasive prompt should follow a basic format. The first paragraph should be an introduction, followed by two to three paragraphs of support, and a conclusion.

Introduction:

- Attention-grabbing opener

- A main idea statement that clearly expresses your opinion

Body:

Supporting Paragraph 1:

— Topic sentence

— Example 1

— Support for example (explanation)

Supporting Paragraph 2:

— Topic sentence

— Example 2

— Support for example (explanation)

Continue with more supporting paragraphs if you have more information.

Conclusion:

• Summary of support

• Action you want the reader to take

Prewriting

While 45 minutes is a significant amount of time, use it wisely. Prewriting should focus on creating well-developed support for your main idea statement. Do not worry so much about how you will start or finish your essay, but focus on what will be included in your body paragraphs.

First, decide whether you will support or be against the idea presented in the prompt. Remember, you need to pick a side! When deciding which side to take, you do not have to pick the side that you personally agree with. Pick the side you feel you can write a better essay on.

To help you decide on which side to select, you may want to create a brief chart showing the pros and cons for each side of the prompt. After you make the chart, see which ideas you feel you can support more and start brainstorming facts and examples about them.

Look at the example below to see how this can be done. Again, time is important, so try to spend only 5 to 7 minutes on prewriting.

Example 1:

Following a string of recent bicycle accidents, the town council did a study. They found that many children were not following the state's bicycle helmet law. Also, they determined that it was rare to see an adult with a helmet on. To encourage the children to wear helmets, the council is deciding on passing a law that will require people, no matter what their age, to wear one.

Write a letter to the town council supporting or disagreeing with this proposed change.

Pros	Cons
Kids would see adults wearing helmets. – 9 out of 10 kids view adults as role models. – If parents think this is important, so will kids. – Positive peer pressure	Kids don't usually act the same as adults.
Adults would be safer – Reduce head injuries	Adults should have the right to choose.
	Helmets for parents and kids could be expensive.

In the chart you can see that there is more information to write about in the "pros" column. Even if you personally disagree with the "pro" side of this subject, consider taking the "pro" side of the issue so you can write your best essay.

Exercise 3 Prewriting:

For the following prewriting exercise, limit yourself to 5 to 7 minutes. Complete the prewriting for each of the following five prompts.

1. Across New Jersey, middle schools have banned students from using cell phones in school. The Board of Education in your town is considering allowing students in your middle school to use cell phones.

Write a letter to your Board of Education stating whether or not you feel that this change will be successful or not.

_____

_____

_____

_____

_____

_____

_____

_____

_____

_____

_____

2. The basketball coach is concerned about his team's poor grades. To combat the low grades, the coach decided to make all the players attend mandatory study sessions twice a week after practice.

Write a letter to your school's newspaper stating the fairness of this new policy.

_____

_____

_____

_____

_____

_____

_____

_____

3. Your school board is thinking about taking away class levels. By having mixed-level classes, they feel it will be better for the self-esteem of the students.

As a student, write a letter to the superintendent explaining your viewpoint of this topic.

_____

_____

_____

_____

_____

_____

_____

4. Recently, your community has become concerned with the overall health of young people. This concern especially focuses on how much sugar students are eating. Their suggestion to the school was to ban clubs from having bake sales and selling candy.

Write a letter to the parents explaining whether you feel that this suggestion is appropriate or not.

_____

_____

_____

_____

_____

_____

5. The Board of Education of your school district has passed a policy that students will be allowed to go home or to a local restaurant for lunch without being signed out by a parent. This is a result of improved grades throughout the school.

Write a letter to the Board of Education stating whether or not this is a wise decision.

_____

_____

_____

_____

_____

_____

_____

Exercise 3 Answers:

Remember, these are possible ideas, not definite answers. Use them as guidance if you are having trouble thinking of ideas and see how they can be shaped into essays.

1.

Pros	Cons
Able to communicate with school in case of an emergency	Not paying attention - When people drive and text, they do not pay attention to the road - Students barely pay attention with no distractions
Get in touch with parents for rides	Texting answers during a test - Answers can be kept in the phone
Use as a calculator if you forget yours	Never know when people are taking photos - Locker room - Post online

2.

Pros	Cons
Create a sense of teamwork - "Everybody is in this together" attitude - Peer tutoring has been successful with homework club in our school.	Some players may not need this extra help.
Overall improvement in the team's grades - Studies have shown that this type of program has boosted grades 2 to 5 points.	Resentment of players with bad grades
Recognize the importance of school work, even if you are an athlete - Homework will be completed at least 2 days a week. - Will show that sports does not replace intelligence	

3.

Pros	Cons
Students can get used to working with different groups of people	Teachers might spend too much time with struggling students; whole class's performance drops – Teacher can spend more time getting kids to pay attention and remind people what assignments they are missing than actually teaching – Assignments might be too easy – Bored
Might be able to learn at own pace	Might actually lower self-esteem of students performing poorly – Someone not understanding a lesson, and needing more help while everyone else moves on – Getting a lower grade than everyone else

4.

Pros	Cons
Kids eating less sugar	Less options for clubs to raise money – How will clubs be able to raise money? – Bake sales are extremely successful
Do not have to worry about food allergies	Limits the freedom people have to make their own choices – If people are worried about their health, it should be their responsibility to take care of themselves.

5.

Pros	Cons
Teach real-world skills.	Students might not come back to class. – Service might be slow and make kids late. – Students might decide to hang out and not go back to class.
Give break from school life.	Restaurants might not like teenage business – Might reduce restaurant's business. because older people might not want to be around teenagers – Might cause a disturbance
	Safety/knowing where kids are – School would not be able to keep track – Kidnapping risk

Writing

As with any other type of timed writing, you should spend the majority of your time on the essay itself. While you are spending 5 minutes on the prewriting, you should spend 30–35 minutes on the actual writing. Remember that your prewriting is not graded or even looked at. You may wish to change some of the ideas you brainstormed if you think of better ones. If that happens, definitely go with the better ideas. The more familiar you are with the framework for persuasive writing, the better. Get in the habit of using the framework to write all of your persuasive pieces.

Also, remember that the majority of your score comes from the content you include in the writing. Start your essay off in a way that will catch the reader's attention. If you use a question, make sure you address it in the second sentence or throughout your essay. The introduction should also have your main idea statement, which clearly has your choice to support or disagree with the prompt.

Make sure all the information you are including supports your main idea and is on topic. The body paragraphs of your essay should convince the reader through examples, facts, or statistics. Finally, end strongly, and do not include any new information in the conclusion. Make sure you tell the reader what you want them to do.

Follow the framework and you should be able to manage your time effectively. Content and organization should be your focus at this stage!

Example 1:

Following a string of recent bicycle accidents, the town council did a study. They found that many children were not following the helmet law. Also, they determined that it was rare to see an adult with a helmet on. To encourage the children to wear helmets, the council is deciding on passing a law that will require people, no matter what their age, to wear one.

Write a letter to the town council supporting or disagreeing with this proposed change.

Dear Town Council:

Have you ever been driving down the street or walking through the park and seen a child who was supposed to be wearing a bike helmet without one? Kids riding bikes without a helmet has been a problem that is not only against the current law, but dangerous. Passing a law to require all people to have to wear helmets will make the entire community safer and encourage children to actually wear one.

The new helmet law will allow young people to see adults wearing a helmet. Children usually look up to adult role models. Sometimes these role models play a sport, sing a song, teach, or are parents. A recent survey found that 9 out of every 10 children respect what an adult role model does. Looking at that survey shows that kids actually pay attention to what adults do. This law will also show that adults value safety. By children seeing this, they will hopefully begin to value the importance of safety. Also, this can be a chance to use positive peer pressure. If someone sees everyone doing something, they may feel the pressure to go along with what everyone else is doing. By making adults wear helmets, kids can definitely see the positive side to wearing a helmet by watching an adult model the correct behavior.

Another reason why this new law is a good idea is because it will protect all bike riders. Head injuries are one of the dangerous and common types of injuries that people have on bikes. Many studies show that helmets greatly reduce the risk or severity of injuries that may occur. Accidents can happen without warning, and having extra protection should be offered to all. Having a law to promote this for adults will surely make all bikers safer.

Having a law to make adults wear helmets can only benefit the entire community. Children, who were previously not wearing helmets, can see adults modeling the correct behavior. Also, forcing adults to wear helmets will make them safer bike riders. Based on this information, the Town Council should support this new law.

Exercise 4 Writing:

For the following exercise, complete one prompt at a time. Time yourself! Try to write the complete prompt in 30 to 35 minutes.

1. Across New Jersey, middle schools have banned students from using cell phones in school. The Board of Education in your town is considering allowing students in your middle school to use cell phones.

Write a letter to your Board of Education stating whether or not you feel that this change will be successful or not.

_____

_____

_____

_____

_____

_____

_____

_____

_____

_____

_____

_____

_____

_____

2. The basketball coach is concerned about his team's poor grades. To combat the low grades, the coach decided to make all the players attend mandatory study sessions twice a week after practice.

Write a letter to your school's newspaper stating the fairness of this new policy.

_____

_____

_____

_____

_____

_____

_____

_____

_____

_____

_____

_____

_____

_____

_____

_____

_____

_____

_____

3. Your school board is thinking about taking away class levels. By having mixed-level classes, they feel it will be better for the self-esteem of the students.

As a student, write a letter to the superintendent explaining your viewpoint of this topic.

_____

_____

_____

_____

_____

_____

_____

_____

_____

_____

_____

_____

_____

_____

_____

_____

_____

_____

_____

4. Recently, your community has become concerned with the overall health of young people. This concern especially focuses on how much sugar students are eating. Their suggestion to the school was to ban clubs from having bake sales and selling candy.

Write a letter to the parents explaining whether you feel that this suggestion is appropriate or not.

_____

_____

_____

_____

_____

_____

_____

_____

_____

_____

_____

_____

_____

_____

_____

_____

5. The Board of Education of your school district has passed a policy that students will be allowed to go home or to a local restaurant for lunch without being signed out by a parent. This is a result of improved grades throughout the school.

Write a letter to the Board of Education stating whether or not this is a wise decision.

_____

_____

_____

_____

_____

_____

_____

_____

_____

_____

_____

_____

_____

_____

_____

_____

_____

_____

Exercise 4 Answers:

Remember, there are no specific right or wrong answers to these prompts. The following sample answers are to be used as guidelines to compare with your own writing.

1. *Dear Board of Education:*

Have you ever been in a library, at the movies, or eating at a restaurant and had your conversation or your quiet interrupted by a cell phone? Allowing cell phones in middle schools can cause a disturbance in classes and possibly infringe on the rights of students. School is a place to learn and focus on doing work, and not be sidetracked. Cell phones would only add another way for already unfocused students to not pay attention.

Looking around any middle school classroom will show a bunch of students engaged in a variety of activities usually not related to the class they are in. Students find it very hard to concentrate on subjects early in the day just after they wake up, after lunch, or late in the day. If someone is hungry or tired it can be extremely difficult to pay attention to what the teacher is saying. Adding cell phones to the class will just add one more distraction. Cell phones can lead to texting when a teacher is trying to give instructions. Texting is a high-tech way to pass notes in class. Think about when people drive and text! Their eyes are never focused entirely on the road if they are texting. Studies have shown that this lack of focus has led to many accidents and even deaths. While students will not die if they are not paying attention in class, the cell phones can lead to lower test grades if students do not pay attention.

Another problem that may occur is cheating during tests. Cell phones could allow for texting in a few ways. First, formulas or information could be entered and saved in phones to be used during the test. Also, test questions and answers can be stored in the phones and given to people who have the test later in the day. While students may discuss test questions and answers already, this will make it easier for them to do it. Also, tests like the SATs and PSATs do not allow cell phones for this reason.

Finally, cell phones can reduce the risk of privacy for all students. Even though camera phones have now added some type of light or noise when a photo is being taken, people may not always notice. While schools are showing assemblies that center around cyber-bullying and the posting of pictures online, this new cell phone allowance will make this a much greater possibility. This situation could create a huge problem in the locker rooms! Also, teachers may have their picture taken without them noticing, and have a fake website made up using their name and picture.

Cell phones in schools are not a good idea. Students will be more easily distracted, cheating may increase, and privacy may decrease. The School Board should not create a policy that will take away from the quality of education students receive.

Say "No!" to cell phones in school.

2. *Dear Editor:*

The best students are not only the ones who do well in class, but also usually are involved in a variety of activities. Student athletes are perfect examples of this type of student. Not only do they get good grades, but also do well on the court. Recently, the basketball coach has been concerned about the grades some of his students are receiving. To try and solve this problem, he has made it mandatory that players attend a study hall twice a week. This is a terrific way to show players that their success in school is just as important as their success after school.

After school study sessions will help improve the teamwork of the players. Having the players meet after practice will show that one person does not make a team and that the success of the team depends on the whole team. When looking at college and professional teams that win championships, the players are often involved in off-the-field or off-the-court activities. When these teams participated in study sessions, community service, or just after practice dinners, it was shown that the commitment to the team and their teammates increased. Getting to know each other off the court actually made the players want to play harder, not wanting to let the team down.

Another positive result of these sessions is that athletes will see the value of education. Athletes are often shown as the "dumb jocks" and labeled as stupid or unintelligent by television shows and movies. If these stereotypes are the only thing athletes see, they may start to believe them. If a coach values the education of his or her players, the team will hopefully start to try just as hard in class as at practice. Sometimes athletes who do great in their sport may feel that that is the only thing they are good in. These study sessions can show that there is a life outside of sports. Many athletes who value education are just as successful at becoming doctors, teachers, and businessmen as they are as players.

Mandatory study sessions will benefit all players; even those who are already doing well in school. Many players might think, "I made honor roll, why should I have to stay and do my homework with the team?" Many players who are dedicated to sports may not have the time in the day to spend on school work. However, if these days are scheduled in, even the best student can benefit by having time to do homework. Studies have shown that teams who have this time scheduled into their week, have the overall team grade go up anywhere between two and five points. Even the best students would want this type of success.

Students have busy lives, especially if they are playing a sport. If the coach teaches the players to be as concerned about their grades as winning, he or she is doing a good job. The athletes and school should appreciate the effort this coach is making. Even though they may not appreciate it now, the coach is giving the student athletes a chance at a more successful future.

3. *Dear Superintendent:*

Schools should give all students the equal chance to do better no matter how smart they are. Having leveled classes such as math foundations, math, and math honors will give students that chance of success. Taking away these classes may sacrifice the overall education of all the students in a class.

Many times people feel that having non-leveled classes will benefit all students. However, this is not always true. Studies show that in a mixed-level class the whole class struggles. For instance, the teacher may not be able to spend an equal amount of time with all students. If the teacher gives an assignment that ¾ of the class understands, but ¼ does not, most likely the teacher will spend most of the time with the students who are struggling. The students who do a good job or seem to get it might only get a quick compliment or decent grade. But, is that student having his or her knowledge increased by just understanding the work?

Another problem that may happen in this same area is that the assignments are made too easy by the teacher so everyone in the class is sure to understand them. When this happens the work might be easy for a lot of the students. If the work is too easy, they will not be challenged. The only way students can really learn something is to have what they already know expanded on. If they are only repeating the same lessons, nothing will ever be learned. Also, if the assignments are too easy, students will become bored. Having a classroom of bored students can result in behavior problems for the class and the school.

The goal of non-leveled classes is to increase a student's self-esteem. However, many times the opposite happens. People often think that the name of a class alone causes students to feel a certain way. An example people use is that students in a foundations class often feel "stupid" because everyone knows what class level they are in. Imagine being a student who struggles in math and is in a class with people who understand and love math. That could actually lower his self-esteem more!

Ronald, a sixth grade student, said, "I know I stink at writing, and I would rather be in a class with other people who have a difficult time. Why would I want to see how much better somebody else in my grade can write than me? That does not help me become a better writer. It just makes me feel worse."

Many people have different views on this topic. The views of the students should be the most important though. So, listen to the students of the school and give them a chance to learn at their own pace in leveled classes.

4. Dear Parents:

The health of children is one of the most important responsibilities of a parent. Along with this though should come teaching wise decision making. Banning bake sales as fund raisers might prevent children from buying cookies once or twice a month, but what will it teach them about decision making? Also, this will make it much more difficult for school organizations to raise the much needed funding that they require to exist.

Just by banning something, children will not learn decision-making It does severely limit the right to make choices for all students. Teenage health is very important, but all the possible dangers or unhealthy activities cannot possibly be removed. So, by removing the bake sales, students will not learn what actually is a healthy amount of cookies a person should eat. Also, many students can eat baked goods without having any negative effects.

Removing the bake sales completely will not teach students the power of good decision making. Students need to learn how to limit themselves. A cookie here and there is not a bad thing! Eating 3 dozen cookies is bad, though. Bake sales, while they do promote the purchase of a cookie or brownie, are not promoting obesity and should not be seen that way.

Finally, banning bake sales will limit the fundraising activities of the clubs that would hold them. Bake sales raise 2 to 3 times more money than all other fundraisers. Megan, a sixth grade student, says, "I would much rather pay 50 cents for a brownie than pay 50 cents for a sticker or button!" Megan shares the same viewpoint as many other students. Hosting a bake sale at a school is also much safer than having students sell something door-to-door or stand outside a supermarket with a can collecting money.

Bake sales are a terrific way for school clubs to raise money. While they do sell goods that may be high in sugar, they should not be seen as enemies of student health.

Support our schools by not banning bake sales!

5. *Dear Board of Education:*

Imagine that you are a business owner who needs to grab a quick lunch before heading back to the office. You walk into the pizzeria, and are met by 25 to 50 sixth, seventh, and eighth graders. Immediately, you would probably be frustrated by the noise and not wait to get your food. Allowing students to go out for lunch is not a good idea and will lead to the frustration of many townspeople and restaurant owners.

The first problem that will be encountered will be getting students back to class on time. Lunch periods are 40 minutes during the busiest time of day for restaurants. If a large number of people choose to go to the same restaurant, service will be slow. This condition can present two problems. One is that students will be marked late coming back to class and may get a detention. The second problem may be that students will recognize that they are running out of time and be forced to go back to class without eating. Either of these dilemmas is not good for students. In addition to this, some students who go out for lunch may decide to cut their afternoon classes and not return to school. The permission to go out will present much more of a temptation for students not to not return to school on time, or at all!

Students going out to local restaurants might also upset owners. While they may welcome business, owners may view teenage business as unwanted business. Older customers may see teenagers as too loud and obnoxious and not want to be in their presence even if they are not behaving that way. As a result, restaurants may actually lose some of their business. Pete, a sixth grader, exclaimed, "Have you ever seen lunchtime in the cafeteria? It's nuts, and that is with lunch ladies and the principal in there. Can you imagine what it would be like out at a restaurant?" Pete echoes many of the same concerns as shop owners. The shop owners are concerned that they are the ones who will have to deal with the disturbance that some teenagers will surely bring, and that is unfair to them.

In addition to the shop owners being unhappy, many parents and teachers will be concerned about the overall safety of students. First, schools will have to take attendance at the beginning of the day, and immediately following lunch. Then, for any students who did not report back, the school will have to locate them. Also, the threat of a student being kidnapped is a real one. Having a student walking by himself or herself to lunch may present an unnecessary risk to safety.

While this opportunity for responsibility may be welcomed by some, it may create more problems than it is worth. Shop owners and townspeople may have a conflict with teenage students. Shop owners may, as a result, lose business. Also, students may decide to cut class. Finally, students' safety may be at risk. Looking at the big picture, the Board of Education should keep students in school for the whole school day.

REVISING YOUR EXPLANATORY AND PERSUASIVE RESPONSES

Following the actual writing of each type of prompt, you should spend 3 to 5 minutes or your remaining time making your response better. This means that you will be rereading your essay more than once. Do not waste this time. First, look for any parts in the essay that are confusing or unclear to you. You may have to cross out sentences that are off-topic or add supporting information. Do not repeat information! Any weakly supported information should be added to. Focus on adding increased details to your body paragraphs, making sure you actually answered the prompt. Words that describe the senses (sight, hearing, smell, taste, and touch), as well as facts, examples, or stories are great ways to do this. Each of these can also be elaborated with specific details and quotations.

Checking your writing to make sure your sentences are complete should be another focus during the revision process of essay writing. Focus on your content and organization rather than if you misspelled a word. Make sure the length of your sentences and your sentence beginnings vary enough to keep the reader interested. This means that you should not have all short sentences or all long sentences. Also, do not start sentences off with the same word. Skim over your writing to look for common or repeated beginnings and replace them.

Overall, the revision process is a time to make your writing as good as possible. Do not panic and do not try to replace your entire essay.

Practice Test 1

Language Arts Literacy

This test is also on CD-ROM in our special interactive NJ ASK6 Language Arts Literacy TestWare®. It is highly recommended that you first take this exam on computer. You will then have the additional study features and benefits of enforced timed conditions and instant, accurate scoring.

Day 1

Section 1

You are now ready to begin Section 1 of the NJ ASK Language Arts Literacy test. You will have 30 minutes to complete the reading passage and the questions that follow. This section will include 9 multiple-choice questions and 1 open-ended response. Work up to the page that has the "stop sign" on the bottom or until time runs out.

If you finish early, check over your work. Remember, you may only check on work in this section.

There are several important things to remember:

1 Read each passage carefully to learn what it is about. You may refer back to the reading passage as often as necessary.

2 Read each question carefully and think about the answer. Then choose or write the answer that you think is best.

3 When you are supposed to write your answers, write them neatly and clearly on the lines provided in your answer folder.

4 When you are supposed to select the answer, make sure you fill in the corresponding circle in your answer folder.

5 If you finish a part of the test early, you may check over your work in that part.

6 If you do not know the answer to a question, skip it and go on. You may return to it later if you have time.

GO ON

The Lives of Penguins

Penguins are amazing creatures whose lives are both fascinating and, at times, bizarre. These flightless creatures are as diverse as the land which they inhabit. Penguins come in a variety of sizes and have many unique features.

A common misunderstanding is that penguins live in only cold places. While certain species do live in Antarctica, many types live on the southern tip of South America, South Africa, and even the Galapagos Islands, which are near the Equator.

[3] Penguins are adapted to live in areas as long as they can swim. Their webbed feet make them excellent swimmers. The webbing always allows the birds to propel themselves underwater after their speedy prey, which includes fish and small squid. Depending on the size of the penguin, larger penguins can hold their breath longer; they can stay underwater averaging from a few minutes to over ten minutes. While a few species of penguins live in warmer climates, many need to survive in frigid water temperatures. To do so, they are protected by a thick layer of feathers. The feathers act like insulation would to a house, keeping the warmth close to the body and the cold water away. The <u>consistency</u> of the dark feathers on the backs of penguins allow for them to dry off quickly. Finally, the eyes make them keen underwater predators. They are extremely useful for spotting food as well as predators that may present danger for the penguins.

In addition to being well-equipped swimmers, penguins are some of the best parents in the animal world. Some penguin species keep the same mate from year to year, which is quite unusual for the animal world. Many scientists have observed that couples are very similar to a married couple. Individual penguins have almost seemed happy when his or her partner has returned after an extended period of time. This dedication to family life is especially seen in the case of the Emperor penguin. From the moment the single egg is laid, one of the parents is continuously with it until the baby is old enough to fend for itself. With these penguins, the father bird bears the frigid Antarctic air to incubate the egg for weeks on end. The egg rests on top of the dad's feet to keep it off the cold ice. A community is formed amongst the father penguins, each huddling together for warmth and protection from the elements.

[5] While the father parents are caring for the egg, the mother birds are at sea feeding and trying to build up enough weight to return to the nesting grounds to care

GO ON

for the newly hatched chick. The return of the mothers is met with great anticipation among the male community. With the return of the females, a shift is made. Now, the females care for the newly hatched chicks, feeding them it and protecting them. Mothers are extremely protective over their babies and fights often break out if others move in too close or try to steal the chick for themselves. During this time, the male penguins march off to sea to <u>replenish</u> much-needed nutrients.

While penguins are one of the most popular exhibits at zoos, in the wild, predators often prey upon these birds. A variety of animals include these flippered creatures as part of their diets. Leopard seals and orcas (killer whales) feast on adult penguins, while large seagulls and eagles have been known to prey on babies in New Zealand.

[7] Even though penguins face some natural dangers, populations are more greatly threatened by a few man-made circumstances. One of the most threatening is habitat destruction. Many breeding grounds, especially those in South America and South Africa, are being encroached upon by beach developments. As buildings and beaches are being built by humans, penguins are forced to share a smaller area with a variety of creatures. If habitats continue to be lost, especially in breeding grounds, the number of penguins being born could be greatly reduced.

Another huge threat to these animals is over-fishing. Over-fishing can lead to food shortages. Their primary food source is fish and squid. The more fish and squid are taken by commercial fishermen, the less there is for penguins to eat. With less of a supply of food, fewer animals can be supported.

Penguins are fascinating creatures built to dart through the ocean currents of the Southern Hemisphere. They are dedicated parents, survivors, and unique to the area in which they live. With conservation awareness for the needs of these flightless birds, they will continue to prosper for generations to come.

GO ON

1 In the 5th paragraph, the word **replenish** means

  A. carry away.

  B. stock up on.

  C. gather up.

  D. chase after.

2 Which of the following situations would be comparable to a penguin's parenting techniques?

  A. A tiger in which the mother cares for and protects the young, while the father is seen as a threat

  B. A salmon that after laying its eggs swims off and dies

  C. A mother whale that feeds and protects its young for the first year of life

  D. A pair of red foxes in which the mother stays with the young to protect them while the male brings food

3 According to the passage, which of the following threats would present the <u>greatest</u> danger to penguins in general?

  A. hotel construction on the tip of South Africa

  B. a pod of hungry orcas

  C. a large seagull circling a penguin breeding area

  D. an increased number of fishermen in the Northern Hemisphere

4 Which of the following details support the idea that penguins are well equipped to be responsible parents?

  A. Finally, the eyes make them keen underwater predators.

  B. Some penguin species keep the same mate from year to year, which is quite unusual for the animal world.

  C. The webbing always allows the birds to propel themselves underwater after their speedy prey, which includes fish and small squid.

  D. The egg rests on top of the dad's feet to keep it off of the cold ice.

5 Which of the following sentences could be added to the 7th paragraph to support the main idea of the paragraph?

  A. A penguin's feathers can also be used to serve as camouflage from predators from the sky and in the sea.

  B. A penguin's life in captivity is often 3 to 4 years greater than that of a penguin in the wild.

  C. Litter, such as plastic, can entangle a penguin and prove to be a life-threatening hazard.

  D. Rodents can be dangerous to penguin colonies as they often eat the eggs before they have a chance to hatch.

GO ON

6 The word **consistency**, found in the third paragraph, means

    A. made up of.

    B. steadiness.

    C. thickness.

    D. elasticity.

7 The author of this passage would <u>most likely</u> agree with which of the following?

    A. Penguins should be protected by placing as many penguins as possible in zoos or aquariums.

    B. Keeping a careful eye on the environmental impact of humans can benefit penguins as well as other animals.

    C. Increased hunting of orcas will be a great way to conserve penguins.

    D. Everyone should attempt travel to where penguins are found to observe them.

8 The main idea of this passage is that

    A. penguins are amazing parents.

    B. penguins eat a variety of sea life.

    C. penguins are built for underwater life.

    D. penguins are fascinating creatures.

9 The passage would <u>most likely</u> appear in which of the following?

    A. an encyclopedia

    B. a wildlife conservation magazine

    C. a travel guide

    D. a magazine that explains how to fish

10 The passage describes penguins as perfect creatures for underwater life based on some of their features.

- Compare the features of a penguin and a human.
- What makes a penguin more suitable for underwater life than a human?

Be sure to include specific examples and details from the passage to support your response.

Write your response in your answer folder.

DO NOT GO ON
UNTIL YOU ARE
TOLD TO DO SO.

Day 1
Section 2

The following section will have you write a response to an explanatory prompt. You will have 25 minutes for this part of the test. A space has been provided for you to use for prewriting and organizing your thoughts. Your prewriting WILL NOT be scored.

The part that will be scored will be your written response. Be careful not to write outside the box because any writing outside the box will not be scored. When you have completed your response, be sure to check over your work in this section only. Do not work on any other sections.

Once the 25 minutes is up, put your pencil down, and close your book.

The guidance counselor of your school has recently started a character education program. The focus of the lesson is to try to teach students to deal with or prevent problems on their own. To get the program started, the counselor has asked you to write an essay based on the following quotation.

> "I've always believed that a lot of the troubles in the world would disappear if we were talking to each other instead of about each other."
>
> —Ronald Reagan

Write an essay explaining what this quote means to you. Be sure to include details and examples.

GO ON

Prewriting:

_____

_____

_____

_____

_____

_____

_____

_____

_____

_____

_____

_____

_____

Write your response in your answer folder.

DO NOT GO ON
UNTIL YOU ARE
TOLD TO DO SO.

Day 1

Section 3

You are now ready to begin Section 3 of the NJ ASK Language Arts Literacy test. You will have 30 minutes to complete the reading passage and the questions that follow. This section will include 9 multiple-choice questions and 1 open-ended response. Work up to the page that has the "stop sign" on the bottom or until time runs out.

If you finish early, check over your work. Remember, you may only check work in this section.

Two Coins

A quarter and a dime, a nickel and a penny. What is it worth? Well obviously 25 cents, 10 cents, 5 cents, and one cent. But can you think of two coins being priceless? Can something seemingly so little be a source of great wealth? The answer to that last question is a definite yes!

The story starts long before I was born. The year was 1941 and my grandfather was about to turn 5 years old. Living in a small apartment in the city with his mother, father, and 4 siblings, money was hard to come by. The rooms were small, the winters were cold, and new possessions were unheard of. Being the second youngest child, grandfather was used to getting <u>hand-me-downs</u> from his older brothers. Even though this would seem like a hardship to me today, he wore these used rags like they were Olympic gold medals. Being the youngest boy, he had great respect for his older brothers as they all went to school during the day and either worked before or after school trying to meet the family's needs. Grandfather did not see much of his father, who was working multiple jobs, doing the best he could. Again, grandfather did not complain because his older brothers were teaching him the ways of the stickball game on the 6th Avenue and 54th Street field.

On May 5, 1941, a penny became the richest piece of currency in the world! "How could that be? It is only worth a penny!" I remember asking my grandfather perplexed. That was the day of my grandfather's birthday. As usual the house was busy

GO ON

with the hustle and bustle of the downtown train station. A birthday cake was being prepared in the kitchen, one of the brothers was running to do a paper route and another was promising birthday punches, but a key person was missing. The birthday boy's dad was at work and ended up absent from the celebration. Grandfather was used to him not being there, but he still hoped. Even though he was allowed to stay up to eleven o'clock, his dad was not home and the dreary, tired eyes of a five-year-old won the battle as grandfather drifted to sleep.

His next memory was being held in two large arms and being carried to bed. As his father tucked him into bed, he slipped a penny into his hands and whispered, "Happy Birthday." As morning came, the shiny new penny marked 1941 still lie clutched in a young boy's hand. After getting dressed, the gift immediately went into his pocket. He did not spend this on candy at the corner store and he did not put it in his ceramic bank in which he was saving up money to buy baseball cards. He just kept it near him every day.

[5] Due to events that were happening in some faraway places that grandfather did not understand at the time, his dad had to join the military a few months later. Later that year, he sadly found out that his 5th birthday was the last one grandfather would ever spend with his dad.

Fast forward 30 years. It is now 1971 and grandfather is just a father at this time. The family moved from the city to the suburbs and my dad recalls a slightly different story of his childhood, but echoing some similarities. My dad had a smaller family growing up. Grandfather remembered how tough it was growing up in hard times with that many people. Like his dad, though, he had to work long hours to support his family. Even though he moved out of the city, he was still forced to work there. So once again, as an ice cream cake was being sliced, and presents opened, there was an eerily familiar absence during a child's 5th birthday. While birthday pleasantries were being celebrated, grandfather was stuck in traffic due to construction, an accident, and a detour.

Following a seemingly never-ending quest to his home, grandfather opened the door to find his son sleeping on the living room floor, the television blaring with the local news, and a pointy "Happy Birthday" hat still attached to his head. That night grandfather carried father to bed and slipped a nickel into his hand while putting a very special penny on his nightstand. To this day, my dad exclaims that these are the two most valuable coins in the world!

GO ON

Fast forward another 30 years. It is now 2001. Ironically, the cycle continued. My 5th birthday was 30 years after my father and 60 years after my grandfather. Again there was a familiar theme to the day's events. As my mom prepared a birthday cake on a seemingly perfect September day, she informed me that dad would not be able to make it tonight because all the flights around the country were canceled. Not until two days later did I see my dad. Little did I know at the time what a valuable gift I would receive.

When he arrived home, he presented me with 3 coins: an old beat-up penny from 1941, a nickel from 1971, and a dime from 2001. We just had a math lesson dealing with money that day, and I knew that I could not even buy a piece of candy with that gift. Needless to say I was annoyed that not only did he miss my birthday, but he gave me a lousy gift.

[10] Fast forward 25 more years. Now that I am a little older, I started to put my gift to use. I keep a very special dime in my pocket to this day as it awaits its new home. On my nightstand lie the two most valuable coins in the world. That penny and nickel represent my family's history! I cannot think of a more valuable 6 cents in the world. While the dime in my pocket may always equal 10 cents to the bank, I am starting to write my history on it. As I sit on my bed, I look at the coins on the nightstand. As I lay down in bed, my wife says good night, and a little baby boy sleeps in his crib a few feet away. I carry the dime for him, and I look at the two coins to remember that I keep one coin to remember where I came from, but the other to remember where I want to be. As I drift off to sleep, I make him a promise. That promise is one I will definitely keep to him five years from now.

The next time you are walking down the street and see a penny, a nickel, a dime, or a quarter, do not just walk past. Don't think that you can't even buy a stamp with any or all of them. Stop and pick it up. Check out the year on the coin. You may be surprised to find that some of the smallest things will leave you with the greatest of memories.

GO ON

1 What event shows that grandfather and father were not angry with their fathers for not being present on their birthdays, but loved them greatly?

A. enjoying the birthday cakes that were made for them

B. staying up late on their birthdays

C. seemingly always being well-behaved for their mothers

D. not buying candy or baseball cards, but saving the coins

2 Throughout the passage, the story presents a number of themes. One of them is to be grateful for the opportunities that you have in life. All of the following events show this except

A. that night grandfather carried father to bed and slipped a nickel into his hand while putting a very special penny on his nightstand.

B. again, grandfather did not complain because his older brothers were teaching him the ways of the stickball game on the 6th Avenue and 54th Street field.

C. while birthday pleasantries were being celebrated, grandfather was stuck in traffic due to construction, an accident, and a detour.

D. to this day, my dad exclaims that these are the two most valuable coins in the world!

3 The main idea of the story can be best described as

A. the struggles a family faces over multiple generations.

B. the narrator explaining what the qualities of a good father are.

C. the disappointment children often feel when they do not get a gift they want.

D. a meaningful experience may not be seen until years after.

4 Paragraph 8 contains the sentence, **"Ironically, the cycle continued."** The following explain the meaning of this sentence except

A. it was not until two days later did I see my dad.

B. little did I know at the time what a valuable gift I would get.

C. she informed me that dad would not be able to make it tonight because all the flights around the country were canceled.

D. my 5th birthday was 30 years after my father and 60 years after my grandfather.

GO ON

5 In the 2nd paragraph, the term **hand-me-downs** tells what about the grandfather's family?

   A. Being clean does not matter to them.

   B. The youngest child wants clothes so he can copy his older brother.

   C. The family cannot afford to spend money on new items for everyone.

   D. The family would rather make their own clothes than buy new ones.

6 At two points in the story, a father is carrying his young son to bed. After putting his child to bed, the father gives the most meaningful gift to his son. Using this information, how do you think the father felt missing his child's birthday?

   A. indifferent

   B. worried

   C. uncaring

   D. saddened

7 The narrator feels like the 2 coins represent history. Which of the following choices <u>best</u> describes the history he is referring to?

   A. significant world events that happened during the year of the coin

   B. the narrator's personal family history

   C. the coins being valuable to coin collectors

   D. the coins that were given as presents being much more rare than normal coins

8 What do you think was the promise that the narrator made to his son?

   A. to buy an expensive gift for his 5th birthday

   B. to tell his son the family history

   C. to make him realize how fortunate he is to get any type of gift

   D. to be present for his son's birthday

9 In the 3rd paragraph, "**with the hustle and bustle of the downtown train station,**" means that

   A. the children and mother were extremely busy trying to do the daily activities of the house.

   B. the parents had no control over the children of the house and they were running around crazily.

   C. as a result of living in the city, the apartment was noisy with outside sounds.

   D. the older brother had to rush off to the train station so he would not miss a train to work.

GO ON

10 Go back to the passage and reread the final paragraph. Use the author's message to explain how an item that may seem worthless may actually have tremendous value to the owner.

In your response use examples from your life as well as the passage to provide support for your answer.

Write your response in your answer folder.

CLOSE YOUR
TEST BOOKLET

Day 2
Section 1

You are now ready to begin Section 1 of the Language Arts Practice Test. You will have 30 minutes to complete the reading passage and the questions that follow. This section will include 9 multiple-choice questions and 1 open-ended response. Work up to the page that has the "stop sign" on the bottom or until time runs out.

If you finish early, check over your work. Remember, you may only check work in this section.

A Living Decoration

What better decoration for any house than to have a living piece of furniture that brightens up not only a room, but also the conversation that fills the air? The perfect example of this type of decoration is a fish tank. Fish tanks are filled with the beautiful and the extraordinary and can fit into any type of budget. While all fish tanks contain water, there are two types of tanks that people can have. Fresh and saltwater aquariums may have some similarities, but equipment, initial set-up, the care involved, cost associated with, and types of fish to choose from varies greatly.

The initial set-up of each type of aquarium has some common components. The first and most important piece of equipment is the tank itself. Tanks can range from being as small as 5 gallons to over 100 gallons. The larger the tank, the more expensive it will be. However, there is not a special tank for fresh water or one for salt water. The most important bit of information to consider with the fish tank is what you can afford and what can fit into the area you want to keep it. After the tank is purchased, the type of filter you will need is the next decision. Filters are extremely important in keeping the tank healthy. A healthy tank translates to healthy fish. The filter is so important because it keeps the water circulating through a series of carbon, cloth-like devices. These devices remove waste, old food, and debris from the tank. In addition to the main filter, you may wish to purchase an under-gravel one. While under-gravel filters can be great in creating an undertow and removing waste from underneath the gravel, they are not necessary if you regularly clean the tank.

GO ON

Once the tank and filter are purchased, a decision will need to be made on a few other devices that will promote a healthy tank. An oxygen pump usually is added to a tank. This is the thing that has bubbles coming out of it into the water. The pump will make sure that the fish and any other living creatures are receiving an acceptable amount of breathable oxygen. In addition to a pump, a heater is necessary to keep the water at a constant temperature warm enough to keep the fish alive. Most of the fish available for purchase come from a tropical environment and need to be cared for accordingly.

While all of the equipment mentioned is the same price whether or not you get a freshwater or saltwater aquarium setup, you will need a few additional items to get a saltwater tank going. Water of a specific salt level needs to be added to a tank. The testing of the water is much more involved with this type of tank than a freshwater one. Because of this, a water-testing kit will also be necessary.

All of this equipment will aid in the general care of the tank. Before any fish are added to the water, the tank must be set up, settled, and properly cared for. A tank should be up and running approximately one week before adding fish just to make sure there are not any problems. This way, the water can get to a consistent temperature that mimics the natural environment of your future fish. Also, testing the makeup of the water level for over a week will let you know if any additives need to be used to make it more balanced. These two areas, if not checked, are the leading cause of death for new fish. With freshwater fish, you have to worry about the temperature more so than anything else. However, saltwater fish are much more sensitive. Not only do owners have to worry about the temperature, but the salt-to-water ratio is also a key factor.

Maintenance for a tank has some common elements, but saltwater owners have a few added items to be concerned about. About once every one or two months, the owner should vacuum the bottom of the tank and change the water. A siphon should be started to get the vacuum going. If doing this by mouth, be careful not to swallow any of the dirty water. By cleaning out the gravel and the water, bacteria and disease will be minimized within the tank. A good strategy to introduce the new water to the tank is to mix the new supply with some of the remaining water in the tank. Also, allow the new water to sit for a while so it is not too cold when added to the tank. Once again, for salt water the level of salt needs to be kept at a balanced level.

GO ON

This may take a few tries before the level is close to the already existing one. If it is not close, do not just assume it will work out; wait until it is correct.

[7] Now to the fun part of owning a fish tank, the fish. Fish come in a huge variety of sizes and shapes. Walking through the aisles of a pet store can be very entertaining. Fish come in so many sizes, personalities, and variations that the decision about which to select can be a challenge. Freshwater varieties are often slightly hardier than their saltwater counterparts. Their diets can be <u>supplemented</u> by flake food the majority of the time as well. Saltwater fish possess some of the most vibrant colors. These fish are beautiful to look at, but need to be monitored to make sure they are reacting well to the conditions. Also, their diets can be slightly more complicated. Many saltwater fish's diets are made up primarily of flake type food, but they also need to be supplemented by items such as brine shrimp.

Fish are living creatures that can even be selected to match the colors of the room. A well-kept fish tank can be the highlight of any room. Even though a tank may be a lot of work at first, at least you do not have to take the fish for a walk in the middle of a frigid night! Having fish can result in a tranquil atmosphere that almost everyone can enjoy. It can be like watching a living television without the reruns!

GO ON

1 The writer of this passage <u>most likely</u> wrote this to

   A. persuade a reader to start a freshwater tank.

   B. persuade a reader to start a saltwater tank.

   C. inform a reader about setting up a fish tank.

   D. entertain the reader by writing about his or her personal troubles setting up a tank.

2 The main reason to wait about a week before adding fish to the aquarium is

   A. to save enough money to buy exactly the fish you want.

   B. to make sure the tank is suitable to support life.

   C. to make sure you actually like having the tank where it is.

   D. to allow you time to clean it before you add fish to it.

3 The main idea of this passage is

   A. while they add a unique feature to any room, a fish tank does present the owner with responsibilities.

   B. fish are much better pets than other animals, because fish can be also seen as decoration for a room.

   C. while fish are a great piece of decoration, they are especially dirty and need constant cleaning.

   D. the unique habits of fish make them a difficult pet to own and should be avoided.

4 Which bit of information supports the statement that saltwater fish require more work than freshwater?

   A. There is not a special tank for freshwater or saltwater.

   B. While all of the equipment mentioned is the same price whether or not you get a freshwater or saltwater aquarium set-up, you will need a few additional items to get a saltwater tank going.

   C. Most of the fish available for purchase come from a tropical environment and need to be cared for accordingly.

   D. Not only do owners have to worry about the temperature, but the salt-to-water ratio is also a key factor.

GO ON

5 Which of the following is NOT a reason to consider when purchasing a tank?

   A. how much money you want to spend

   B. where you want to keep the tank

   C. whether you will have a saltwater or freshwater aquarium

   D. how many gallons of water it can hold

6 All of the following characteristics influence the overall health of an aquarium and the fish inside it <u>except</u>

   A. the food that makes up a fish's diet.

   B. how much oxygen is in the water.

   C. the temperature of the water.

   D. how much money the fish costs.

7 In the 7th paragraph, the word **supplemented** means

   A. completed by.

   B. having used an imitation.

   C. to have purchased.

   D. decreased by.

8 The title of the passage, "A Living Decoration," refers to

   A. the plants that are used to decorate a fish tank.

   B. the fish that are used to increase the color of a fish tank.

   C. the fact that a fish tank contains living creatures, but can be used to beautify a room in a house.

   D. the gravel and other ornaments used to liven up the barrenness of the tank.

9 The passage would most likely recommend fish tank ownership to

   A. a person who works during the week, but is home on the weekends.

   B. a family that has a new baby as well as 2 dogs.

   C. a little boy in third grade.

   D. a person about to move to a small apartment.

GO ON

10 Throughout the passage, some similarities and differences of freshwater and saltwater fish ownership are discussed along with some suggestions for the care of this type of pet.

Write a response that explains which of the two choices you would select if you were about to become the owner of a new fish tank.

Be sure to include specific examples and details from the passage as well as your personal experiences.

Write your response in your answer booklet.

DO NOT GO ON
UNTIL YOU ARE
TOLD TO DO SO.

Day 2

Section 2

For the persuasive writing section of the test, you will have 45 minutes to complete your answer to the prompt. A space has been provided for you to use for prewriting and to organize your thoughts. Your prewriting WILL NOT be scored.

The part that will be scored will be your written response. Be careful not to write outside the box because any writing outside the box will not be scored. When you have completed your response, be sure to check over your work in this section only. Do not work on any other sections.

Once the 45 minutes is up, put your pencil down, and close your book.

The vice principal of your school has been noticing that after-school detentions are not being seen as punishment by many of the students who are receiving them. As a result, the vice principal is looking into the possibility of holding Saturday morning detention sessions. The vice principal is trying to see whether or not the school community feels that this would improve behavior amongst troublesome students.

Write a letter to the vice principal in which you support or oppose the idea to add Saturday morning detention sessions to your school district. Make sure that you use examples and other evidence to support your decision.

GO ON

Prewriting:

Write your response in your answer booklet.

DO NOT GO ON
UNTIL YOU ARE
TOLD TO DO SO.

Day 2
Section 3

You are now ready to begin Section 3 of the NJ ASK Language Arts Literacy test. You will have 30 minutes to complete the reading passage and the questions that follow. This section will include 9 multiple-choice questions and 1 open-ended response. Work up to the page that has the "stop sign" on the bottom or until time runs out.

If you finish early, check over your work. Remember, you may only check work in this section.

The Magic Bus

Ernest always had an imagination that sometimes took him far away from reality. What was seen through his eyes was amazing, as he often traveled to faraway places without ever leaving his home or school. As he lay in bed, a mission of exploration and conquest popped into his head. How was he going to sleep now? His mind was racing with his secret goals he would have to achieve. He immediately thought that if he were to travel to a faraway place, he would have to learn their language. Luckily for him, he had a translator.

He snuck out of bed and went to his explorer's kit. After some searching, he found what he was looking for. In his speckled, marbled notebook was a list of common phrases that would help him tomorrow. He attached his book light to the side of his bed, crept underneath it, and began to review these terms. He had to be hidden because he did not want this secret language discovered or too many questions would be asked. As Ernest read "'I' before 'e' except after 'c'" he heard, "Ernest, get to bed! You have school tomorrow and it's late!" He thought he'd better get to sleep before the secret words are discovered.

As he awoke the next morning, he knew a breakfast was in order. He did not want to risk going to the faraway land on an empty stomach. After having pancakes, with butter and syrup, he kissed his mom good-bye. After all, he was not sure when the next time he would see her would be. "Have a great day, Sweetie," she cheerily said as Ernest left the house.

GO ON

He walked to the launch site as an astronaut walked to the spaceship. As Ernest arrived at the location he was met by strange creatures. These creatures looked very similar to him. This would make it easy for him to blend in. As he approached the crowd, he heard them whispering. Ernest could barely hear their muffled grunts and sounds. Through his deciphering skills he was able to make out, "I wonder if he is going to annoy the teacher today with one of his bizarre stories. Yikes, that kid is just weird." As Ernest was listening, one of the creatures glanced back over its shoulder. Ernest immediately stared the other way. He could not be discovered as an outsider this early in his mission. Anyway, he saw his vessel approaching.

[5] "Hurry up you misfits! We have 3 other stops to make! You think I got all day?" loudly shouted the captain of the vessel. Ernest thought that what he was yelling must be the greeting of this foreign land. As the big yellow vessel blasted off with a rumble, a black cloud was <u>emitted</u> behind it. Ernest was lucky to find a seat by himself. This way, he would be able to observe the ways of these strangers and try to file in with them as they arrived at their location. At the last stop, a friendly creature sat next to Ernest. His name was Carl. Carl was quite chatty and told Ernest absolutely everything about what he ate for dinner last night. It seemed Carl was quite fond of food. Ernest felt fortunate to have one of these foreign creatures befriend him. Going to a different land can be extremely intimidating at times. As Carl was wrapping up what he had for dessert, the captain shouted, "Everybody out!" That must have been their way of saying good-bye.

As the two entered the brick building, Ernest was talking about his special training missions that would prepare him for any type of alien attack. Carl was familiar with that type of training, but commented that he accidentally broke his controller and then misplaced his video game. Carl noticed and said, "Ernest, where are you going? You walked past your classroom!"

"Oh, thanks, buddy," Ernest said. He then went to his seat. As he arrived at the seat, the "teacher," as they called her, asked for Ernest's documents. It was as if she was speaking a foreign language even though some of the words sounded familiar.

"Ernest, your homework, where is it? Ugh, just give me your folder. See? It's right here! Was that so hard?" commanded the "teacher." The inhabitants of these foreign places were all so bossy. Luckily, he had his documents in order or who knows what might have happened! As all this activity was going on around him, Ernest began to

GO ON

think of what training mission he would have to complete tonight just in case those aliens ever came. As he was thinking, a bell rang and the teacher yelled "Lunchtime."

Back where the food was being served, Ernest ran into Carl. He remembered that Carl seemed to be an expert on food so he followed his lead so he would not stick out or eat something poisonous. He saw something that looked like pizza his mom would make, and Carl grabbed 3 pieces of it, so it must be a good choice. When they got back to the table, Ernest immediately dove into his food, as his day's travels made him hungry. To his delight, this tasted exactly like the food back home. Before he knew it, they were being shipped back to their separate places.

[10] When Ernest returned, the "teacher" immediately barked out a series of orders. "Clear your desks. I will be passing out paper for your spelling tests. After I read the words, you will need to spell them correctly. Then choose 5 and write sentences that show the meaning of the words. After you hand your test in, write down your homework. Remember, there is no talking. Also, pay attention because we do not have time to waste. The day is almost over." All this talking made Ernest's head feel like it was about to explode! This must be the "teacher's" way of torturing outsiders and to find out who they are as they hid in the class. Ernest knew he'd better focus. As the words were read, a feeling of luck came over Ernest. These were the words he looked over last night!

After the "teacher" stopped reading words, Ernest noticed that the yellow vessel returned to where it dropped everyone off in the morning. Unfortunately, he was spotted! "Ernest!!! If you do not finish your test, you will not leave until you do! Do I make myself clear?" Yikes, what would happen if he were to miss the vessel back home? Who knows what kind of torture would await him after school. He did not want to think about that, so he knew he needed to focus again.

Luckily, he finished just as the bell rang. He grabbed his belongings and raced to the vessel. Before he knew it, he was back home and talking to his mother. Immediately, he was asked, "How was school today?" Where should he even begin his adventure he thought as he bit into a warm, freshly baked chocolate chip cookie. Ah, it was good to be back home!

1 The setting can <u>best</u> be described as

    A. taking place in the past in a foreign land.

    B. occurring in the future during an alien invasion.

    C. during the present time at a school.

    D. during the present on a vacation to a unique destination.

2 The main idea of the entire passage is

    A. sometimes an active imagination can help you deal with unpleasant activities and make them bearable

    B. a good friend is important for everyone to have.

    C. a home-cooked meal can make anyone feel better after a bad day.

    D. when traveling to a foreign place, you should always be prepared and keep your guard up.

3 Which of the following activities would <u>most likely</u> interest Ernest?

    A. participation in an after-school play

    B. reading a science fiction story in a book

    C. joining a sports team

    D. helping his mom with household chores

4 In the 5th paragraph, the word **emitted** means

    A. held in.

    B. threw around.

    C. to have taken off.

    D. to have given off.

5 Which of the following details supports the statement that Ernest does not have a lot of friends at school?

    A. "Hurry up you misfits! We have 3 other stops to make! You think I got all day?"

    B. He could not be discovered as an outsider this early in his mission.

    C. Ernest was lucky to find a seat by himself.

    D. "Ernest, your homework, where is it? Ugh, just give me your folder. See? It's right here! Was that so hard?"

GO ON

6 Which of the following can <u>best</u> be used to describe Ernest after reading the 2nd paragraph?

A. Ernest is studious and schoolwork is extremely important to him.

B. Ernest is an overachiever who wants to do well on everything.

C. Ernest is creative and uses this to his advantage.

D. Ernest is unorganized, but usually gets his work done.

7 How do most of the students feel about Ernest?

A. friendly and accepting of him

B. impressed and interested in him

C. annoyed by his actions and try to ignore him

D. annoyed by his actions and try to make him change

8 Was the "teacher" trying to "torture" Ernest? Which statement <u>best</u> describes what was happening in Paragraph 10?

A. She was trying to figure out which of her students did not belong in the classroom.

B. She gave too many directions at once, and Ernest could not focus.

C. She was trying to cause Ernest pain by using her powers as the alien.

D. She was making sure her students were following directions by slowly reviewing the day's goals.

GO ON

9 The main conflict Ernest faced throughout the passage was

    A. getting through an activity he did not enjoy.

    B. trying to pass an extremely difficult test.

    C. getting the courage to tell a friend something difficult without hurting the friend's feelings.

    D. trying to find his way back home after getting lost.

10 This passage showcases the imagination of Ernest. Many times he is living more in his created world than his actual world.

Does having an active imagination help or hurt a person in handling a problem he or she is having?

Use information in the passage as well as your experiences to provide support for your answer.

Write your response in your answer booklet.

CLOSE YOUR
TEST BOOKLET

Practice Test 2

Language Arts Literacy

This test is also on CD-ROM in our special interactive NJ ASK6 Language Arts Literacy TestWare®. It is highly recommended that you first take this exam on computer. You will then have the additional study features and benefits of enforced timed conditions and instant, accurate scoring.

Day 1

Section 1

You are now ready to begin Section 1 of the NJ ASK Language Arts Literacy test. You will have 30 minutes to complete the reading passage and the questions that follow. This section will include 9 multiple-choice questions and 1 open-ended response. Work up to the page that has the "stop sign" on the bottom or until time runs out.

If you finish early, check over your work. Remember, you may only check work in this section.

There are several important things to remember:

1 Read each passage carefully to learn what it is about. You may refer back to the reading passage as often as necessary.

2 Read each question carefully and think about the answer. Then choose or write the answer that you think is best.

3 When you are supposed to write your answers, write them neatly and clearly on the lines provided in your answer folder

4 When you are supposed to select the answer, make sure you fill in the corresponding circle in your answer folder.

5 If you finish a part of the test early, you may check over your work in that part.

6 If you do not know the answer to a question, skip it and go on. You may return to it later if you have time.

GO ON

Writer's Block

Janet and Haley sat in the Journalism Club meeting after school. The advisor of the club, Mr. Copperstein, was discussing what it meant to write a good article and that the newspaper needed good articles for the last issue of the year. Everybody seemed to have an idea about what to write for their articles. "I am going to write on the boy's baseball and girl's softball seasons," commented Earl, the editor.

"I'm going to write one on the 8th Grade Dance," said Marissa.

"6th Grade Orientation, editorial on going to high school, new vending machines in the cafeteria, school field trip," were all being yelled out by various members. While all of these were decent ideas, Mr. Copperstein just did not seem overly impressed or excited about any of them. He was always looking for that special story, that "something" that would have readers remembering it long after they threw away the newspaper. Janet and Haley had absolutely no idea what topic they wanted to write about. It was not exactly easy to come up with a newsworthy story. After all, they were in middle school, and it was not like they lived in an exciting city. The mail being late would be considered an exciting day here in Newtonville.

"Well girls, what's it going to be? If you can't think of anything, I can come up with an assignment for you," dryly commented the advisor.

[5] "That's okay! We will think of something. Can we have until Monday?" asked Janet in a quick way.

"Well, if you must. But Monday is the absolute latest if you want an article in the paper and we need another topic for the paper you know," was his response.

Even though it was only Thursday, they still had no idea what to do, but they certainly did not want Mr. Copperstein selecting a topic for them. On their walk home they imitated his distinctly serious voice to discuss the awful topic he would probably assign to them. As they were amusing themselves mocking their newspaper coach, they approached the part of the walk home they hated the most. To get home, they had to walk down a dead end dirt road, past a desolate house's property, and meet up with Main Street on the opposite side of the property.

GO ON

The house was set back from the dirt road, and the conifers did a great job concealing it most of the year with their green, piney branches. The odd, creepy thing about the house was that there was always a huge number of perching crows all around the property. The constant "cawing" that broke the silence of the area made the girls speed up the pace at which they were walking. Someone did live in the house, but the story behind the person was never known. However, the resident was known as "Bird Man" and "Man of the Trees." Stories were told that the man was a convicted criminal or insane. It was rumored that he had not left the house in over 20 years.

As they hustled past the house, a gust of wind blew Haley's hat over the fence into the yard. As the two girls tried to peek over the fence to see just how far the hat had gone, something scared the crows and the girls sprinted towards Main Street. By the time they were home, they chuckled as they tried to catch their breath from all the running. Janet and Haley agreed that they would call each other if they thought of anything.

[10] The next day as they were walking home, Haley's hat was perched on the post with the crows high above. Inside the hat, neatly scrawled on a small piece of lined paper, was clipped a note. *"I believe you lost this! I did not see who you are, but I hope you find your lost belonging. I know just how bad it can be to lose something. Sincerely, Paul the Bird Man"*

Haley was happy that her hat was returned, but she was also intrigued by the contents of the message. The message seemed friendly enough, but it also had a sense of sadness. Immediately a light bulb went off. Would Janet consider interviewing the "Bird Man" as the topic for the article? Of course they would have to actually get up the courage to go behind the fence. When the idea was presented to Janet, she was immediately excited. Janet started talking about horror movies and how they could end up making the news themselves if they never made it out of the "Bird Man's" house alive! Haley just stood there shaking her head. She was always amazed at what a drama queen her best friend could be. After briefly discussing their idea, they knew they would have to tell Mr. Copperstein.

As they entered the classroom, Mr. Copperstein was asleep with his glasses hanging off one ear. The girls decided to just leave him a note and complete the assignment on their own. On the way home from school, the girls left a note exactly where the hat

GO ON

173

was placed. It read, *"Paul, thank you so much for returning my hat! My friend, Janet, and I were wondering if we could come by tomorrow to thank you in person at around three o'clock? Well, we will knock on the gate, and if you want to talk to us, you can."*

Much to their surprise, the gate was opened upon their arrival. As they entered, they were amazed at the beauty of the backyard. Behind the conifers lies a yard of tulips, roses, raspberry bushes, and just a kaleidoscope of colors. Beyond the colors were a few small cages with what looked like injured crows hopping around in them. At a small table in the middle of the yard sat an old man in a wheelchair with a warm, welcoming smile on his face. "Well, hello girls! I am glad that you got your hat. Thank you so much for your kind note." The girls were awestruck by the beauty that surrounded them.

Over the next hour or so, Paul politely answered questions from both girls. He chuckled at the rumors that surrounded his life, explained how his life changed the day he lost use of his legs, and even discussed the crows. Not only was he a kind old man, but he had lived and was still living a fascinating life. The reporters were not only learning about Paul, but were also learning a great deal about the town in which they lived. Paul was a witness to Newtonville's history and told it with the passion that authors would use to describe a book they had just proudly finished writing. When Janet and Haley realized the time, they knew their parents would be worried. They both shook Paul's hand and asked permission to print their afternoon's conversation in the school newspaper. He said he would be honored if that were to happen, but they had to promise to get him a copy.

[15] Mr. Copperstein, the rest of the newspaper staff, and the town in general, were amazed at the terrific article that was published. For someone who lived in town his entire 80 plus years, few people were ever inside Paul's fence. "Behind the Fence, Bird Man's Paradise" was responsible for the most newspaper sales the school had ever seen. More importantly, something that was once lost was finally returned to its rightful owner.

GO ON

1 Why do you think Mr. Copperstein was not as excited as the students about the selections they suggested for their newspaper?

   A. He is a person who goes out of his way to make the lives of the students difficult.

   B. The topics chosen were ordinary and did not show any creativity.

   C. Mr. Copperstein gave the students the ideas for their assignments, so none of their articles were new to him.

   D. All the topics were generally the same, so he realized the students had only come up with one topic.

2 At the beginning of the story, the scene outside of The Bird Man's house can <u>best</u> be described as

   A. an oasis of beautiful flowers.

   B. a welcoming home of a lonely old man.

   C. a dangerous home of a crazed criminal.

   D. an ominous scene hidden from the eye.

3 When Haley describes Janet as a **drama queen**, what does she mean?

   A. Janet is bossy and has to be in charge.

   B. Janet is nosey and always has to know everything that is happening.

   C. Janet overreacts and thrives on getting attention.

   D. Janet is someone who brags and always has to be the best.

4 Newtonville can <u>best</u> be described as a town that

   A. nothing ever happens in, so the townspeople gossip to pass the time.

   B. is in the middle of a forest, so it supports a variety of wildlife.

   C. is made up of hardworking citizens who focus on making the community better.

   D. is private and unwelcoming to outsiders.

GO ON

5 Which of the following details would lead the girls to believe that Paul was not a threat to their safety?

   A. For someone who lived in town his entire 80-plus years, few people were ever inside Paul's fence.

   B. When Janet and Haley realized the time, they knew their parents would be worried.

   C. The message seemed friendly enough, but it also had a sense of sadness.

   D. As they entered, they were amazed at the beauty of the backyard.

6 Which of the following choices would be the <u>best</u> theme for the selection?

   A. Do not trust a stranger, because you do not know what his or her intentions may be.

   B. Always walk home with a friend because he or she can help you if something bad happens.

   C. The best ideas are often right in front of you; you just have to be brave enough to try to get them.

   D. Outward appearances do not always present a clear picture of the true beauty a person or thing may have on the inside.

7 All of the following may be reasons why Paul signed his letter, "*Paul The Bird Man*" <u>except</u>

   A. he did not want to reveal his true identity.

   B. he was proud to care for the crows and welcomed the name.

   C. he was not sure if the girls would know who the letter was from if he just wrote "Paul".

   D. he found some of the rumors told about him amusing.

8 Why do you think Paul kept injured crows in his backyard?

   A. He was the reason they were injured, so he felt bad.

   B. Like the crows, he was injured and felt a bond with them.

   C. If he did not keep the crows, he would lose his nickname.

   D. If the crows were let go, they would damage his garden.

GO ON

9 The last paragraph comments that *"More importantly, something that was once lost was finally returned to its rightful owner."* What was returned to Paul?

   A. a piece of clothing that he lost long ago

   B. a place in the spotlight as he was the star of the article

   C. a sense of belonging to the world outside his fence

   D. an injured crow that escaped that Paul was caring for

10 In the passage, Paul commented that *"I know just how bad it can be to lose something."* Think of a time when you lost something important to you. What was he trying to say on the note he left in the hat? What does it feel like if that lost item was able to come back to you?

Use examples from the passage or details from your experiences to support your answer.

Write your response in your answer folder.

DO NOT GO ON
UNTIL YOU ARE
TOLD TO DO SO.

Day 1
Section 2

The following section will have you write a response to an explanatory prompt. You will have 25 minutes for this part of the test. A space has been provided for you to use for prewriting and organizing your thoughts. Your prewriting WILL NOT be scored.

The part that will be scored will be your written response. Be careful to not write outside the box because any writing outside the box will not be scored. When you have completed your response, be sure to check over your work in this section only. Do not work on any other sections.

Once the 25 minutes is up, put your pencil down, and close your book.

Many people look to sports figures, movie stars, musicians, family members, and teachers for guidance. Many of these people are viewed as heroes and are looked up to by many.

Think of the qualities a hero possesses. In an essay, explain what these qualities are and why they are important to you. Be sure to use examples and details to show why these qualities are commendable.

GO ON

Prewriting:

_____

_____

_____

_____

_____

_____

_____

_____

_____

_____

_____

_____

Write your response in your answer folder.

DO NOT GO ON
UNTIL YOU ARE
TOLD TO DO SO.

You are now ready to begin Section 3 of the NJ ASK Language Arts Literacy test. You will have 30 minutes to complete the reading passage and the questions that follow. This section will include 9 multiple-choice questions and 1 open-ended response. Work up to the page that has the "stop sign" on the bottom or until time runs out.

If you finish early, check over your work. Remember, you may only check work in this section.

The Changing Strike Zone

Baseball of the 1940s and baseball of the 1990s are similar in a number of ways, but the game is also different now. In both decades, baseball has had to overcome a sudden loss of popularity, and in both decades it did. Both decades were also dominated by the New York Yankees, a ball club with as storied a history as the game of baseball itself. However, the game of baseball has undergone a series of changes as well in the last fifty years. The game that was once known as the "National Pastime" has now become a worldwide sport. Another change can be found in the star players of each decade. Baseball is a game whose foundations remain the same, but those foundations have led to a series of changes over time.

Baseball of the 1940s and the 1990s, separated by a half century, have many factors in common. Three strikes is still an out, three outs and the teams change their positions in the field, the bases are still the same distances apart, and the team with the most runs wins the game. In addition to these details, baseball had to recover from a serious problem in both decades. In the forties, a large percentage of fans were taken away from the game of baseball because of World War II. Since men made up the majority of those at games, attendance dropped as men were drafted and went to war. Aside from fans being drafted, many of the game's stars were taken away from the game. Players such as Ted Williams and Joe DiMaggio lost up to four years of their careers to serve their country. After the war was over, interest in the game increased dramatically because of the new innovation of televised games.

The need to rebound from lack of interest was not seen again until the nineties. The lack of interest in that decade was the result of a labor strike in 1994 that plagued baseball for two seasons. When the season was canceled, many fans vowed

GO ON

180

never to return to the game they once adored. However, when baseball returned, so did the fans. The damage took a couple years to fully repair, but through a series of promotions and public relations pitches, such as throwing almost all foul balls to fans, they returned. Both rebounds showed baseball's resilience and its ability to overcome a sudden decrease in interest and remain as popular a sport as it has always been.

Another similarity for both decades has been the dominance of the New York Yankees franchise. During the 1940s, the Yankees won four World Series while appearing in five. Aside from being a dominating ball club, one of the game's most dominating players roamed centerfield at Yankee Stadium. Joe DiMaggio, "The Yankee Clipper," was one of the biggest stars of the decade and illustrated this with his fifty-six game hitting streak in 1941.

This dominance recurred in the 1990s. The Yankees of the 1990s finished the decade by winning three of the final four World Series. Centerfield was once again roamed by one of the game's biggest stars, Bernie Williams. The 1998 Batting Champion helped to lead his team to the title of "The Team of the Decade" by baseball analysts. The popularity of the Yankees suggests that many franchises have as loyal of a following as the game of baseball itself. While this is only one franchise, it has been the only one to remain successful in its original city.

While the game in the 1940s and the 1990s has many similarities, it also has an equal number of differences. The game was restricted to the United States during the decade of the forties. This could be because of the isolationist policy of the country during the 1930s. The United States was interested in little other than breaking out of the Great Depression. As a result of this policy, the game, along with many other products and ideas of the United States, were not <u>exported</u>. With the outbreak of World War II, the interest in baseball moved to the background.

In the 1990s, good economic times helped bring about the exportation of the game, making it truly international. It is now common to see baseball being played in Japan and the Middle East, as well as many Central and South American countries. With this expansion, baseball's nickname might need to be changed from the "National Pastime" to the "Global Pastime."

However, the most extreme change in the game of baseball can be seen by looking at the cultural and social background of its players. The stars of the forties were of

GO ON

white Italian or other European ancestry and their parents were usually mid-western farmers or Californian fishermen. This description fits both the immigration and segregation patterns of the country. The majority of people, who had been coming to the country during this era, in an effort to better their lives or to escape disaster, were from the European nations. Also, baseball, like the rest of the country, was governed by the so-called separate but equal policy. While white ballplayers prospered in the Major Leagues, African American players were forced to barnstorm in the Negro Leagues.

A completely opposite ethnic and social composition can be found in the nineties. Players come from a melting pot of nations including the United States, Japan, the Dominican Republic, and Cuba. Baseball in both decades reflected changing times and conditions found in the country. This ability to adapt to changing times has kept the game popular. This ability will aid baseball to remain a popular sport as times continue to change.

The game of the forties and the game of the nineties have many similarities. In both decades, a rebound in interest was made to preserve the existence of the game. Also, New York Yankee teams dominated the sport. But, even with these similarities, baseball is an extremely different game today. It is a much more global game today compared with what it was in the forties. The ethnic and social backgrounds of the most popular players have changed completely. The foundation of the game of baseball remains stable, but its appearance has been restructured. While keeping certain aspects the same, it is also a sport that is able to represent the changes in the United States over the same period of time.

GO ON

1 According to the passage, baseball of the forties and nineties have all of the following in common <u>except</u>

   A. the Yankees being a dominant team.

   B. who was allowed to play the game.

   C. having an event causing fans to lose interest.

   D. fans returning to the game after a departure.

2 Baseball is called the "National Pastime" because

   A. it is a popular game throughout the country.

   B. it is the favorite sport around the world.

   C. teams are often made up of players from the same nation.

   D. whenever trades took place with another country, the rules of the game would also be shared.

3 In this passage, **isolation** means

   A. being locked away.

   B. trading with another country.

   C. not being a fan of baseball.

   D. removing oneself from the events of the world.

4 Which of the following statements would be true if it were to be added to the passage?

   A. Bernie Williams would have helped the Yankees win more championships if he did not have to fight in World War II.

   B. The Yankees have called New York home from the moment they became a team until today.

   C. Major League Baseball star players of the forties were able to relate to a series of diverse groups.

   D. Baseball today has fewer fans than it did in the past.

GO ON

183

5 Which of the following events would be the <u>main</u> reason why baseball switched from being a primarily American event to a world event?

   A. the decrease in the popularity of soccer around the world

   B. the fight for equal rights throughout the country

   C. the improvement of technology such as television and, eventually, computers

   D. the end of World War II

6 Which of the following statements would the author <u>most likely</u> agree with?

   A. Changes in the game resulted in fans leaving.

   B. Changes in the game were made in an effort by teams to make more money.

   C. Changes are rare throughout the history of the game.

   D. Changes reflect events occurring in the United States.

7 The word **exported** means

   A. to have changed.

   B. to have been brought into an area.

   C. to have been sent out of an area.

   D. to have been sent by ship.

8 Looking at the reasons why baseball lost fans in the 1940s and 1990s, what is an accurate statement that can be made?

   A. Baseball, in both decades, had little control over its success.

   B. Baseball did not have to work as hard to get back the support of fans in the 1990s as it did in the 1940s.

   C. The 1940s had much better players, so fans do not find the game as exciting anymore.

   D. Baseball lost fans because of events it could not control in the 1940s; however, the same was not true for the 1990s.

GO ON

9 The statement, *"The game of baseball has had its foundation remain stable, but its appearance restructured,"* means that

    A. change affects everything, no matter how hard people try to keep it the same.

    B. the creation of a problem creates more change than a solution does.

    C. even though everything may change, certain aspects of life will always remain the same.

    D. change confuses the majority of people and causes them to lose interest.

10 Change is often seen as a negative event. Using the case of baseball and any examples you may have, explain whether change is a positive or negative event.

Write your response in your answer folder.

CLOSE YOUR
TEST BOOKLET

Day 2

Section 1

You are now ready to begin Section 1 of the NJ ASK Language Arts Literacy test. You will have 30 minutes to complete the reading passage and the questions that follow. This section will include 9 multiple-choice questions and 1 open-ended response. Work up to the page that has the "stop sign" on the bottom or until time runs out.

If you finish early, check over your work. Remember, you may only check work in this section.

Buster the Great

Katie lies asleep. The morning sun crept through the blinds like a burglar into an unsuspecting house. The sun warms the room and begins to lighten her face. Tranquility is the best way to describe the room. As Katie rolls over, a blast of noise erupts out of the alarm clock. With a swift punch, the snooze button is hit.

At the foot of the bed is another sleeper. With the peacefulness disturbed, Buster slowly begins to get the sleepiness out of his head. A yawn, then a shake, and then a scratch behind the ear. The usual morning routine is under way. With the clinking of his collar, this small, brown dog begins to make his trek to his owner's side. He plops down right next to her head, gives a little sniff, and relaxes again. The peacefulness is once again disturbed by the blaring noise of the alarm clock. This time, the smash on the snooze button is a little too forceful and it knocks the alarm clock to the floor. Katie quickly rolls to the other side of the bed, and Buster has to jump out of the way.

Buster, still looking for some attention, is about ready to make his morning trip outside. Gently, he tries to get Katie to take him outside with a sniff to the ear. Nothing, Nada, Zilch! She is already back to sleep. Buster really is getting impatient as he needs to get his day started, so he starts Katie's day with a whack to the face. "Buster! No, I do not like that. Let's go, time for you to go outside." As Katie gets out of bed, she realizes just how cold it is. Winter in New Jersey's Skylands Region, in the northwestern corner of the state, can be quite unpleasant. As she wobbles down the stairs, her eyes barely opened, memories of her pillow and warm sheets fill her head.

As the door opens, Buster races outside. The frigid air rushes in and causes Katie to shiver. As she watches her dog hop around the backyard, her mind recollects a very special

GO ON

moment in her life. Immediately, the New Jersey kitchen transforms to a dog pound in Boston. A recent move had relocated Katie into a small apartment in this small city made famous by Fenway Park, clam chowder, and the Revolutionary War. This move left Katie starting a new school, living in a new place, and making new friends. She never anticipated her best friend would be of the four-legged variety.

[5] At the pound, a wise, older collie guarded the entrance behind the door of his cage. "Nope," Katie thought to herself, "too big." Next, was a fat, toothy bulldog with a stuffed unicorn clenched between his jaws. "Nope, too ugly." After wandering up and down the aisles, she noticed that some of the cutest creatures were already adopted. "Darn it," she thought to herself, knowing that she should have gotten there immediately after she heard about the pet adoption. Just as she was about to leave and was walking past the last cage, something caught her eye. This small, toy poodle came meandering over close to the cage door. This brown guy had to be the runt of the litter. "Little, slightly pathetic looking, but PERFECT!" thought Katie. She could not fill out the paperwork quick enough.

Over the next four years in Boston, Katie began to remember that many people came into her life and left. While the people were not always around, one friend definitely was always by her side. When she was sick and feeling pathetic with the flu, Buster was by her side, when she was homesick for New Jersey, there was Buster. He was like a guardian angel, always bouncing at the perfect time. With a lick or a sniff, Katie would immediately feel better.

While friends would often ask favors or help with homework, or when having to go out on a rainy night to pick up food for company, Buster simply wanted a scratch on the head or a tasty treat. Katie began to remember how Buster would scratch at the inside of the apartment door whenever he would hear the jingling of her keys as she struggled to get them out of her pocketbook to unlock the door. "Oops!" After an <u>instantaneous</u> trip back into her New Jersey kitchen, Katie realizes that Buster is actually scratching at her kitchen door so he can get back into the warm house. As soon as the door is open an inch, he bolts in with a wag of his tail. He prances through the kitchen, almost grinning as his busy morning is pretty much complete. His trip through the kitchen concludes with a quick detour to his water bowl before ending up on his pillow in the sun.

Seeing the smile on both of their faces, it is easy to tell that they are perfect for each other. While friendship or anything else in life may never be seen as perfect, anyone who is welcomed into the lives of these two would immediately feel a sense of belonging and luck. Friends can come in a variety of sizes and shapes. They can be obvious choices or come straight out of nowhere. A good friend is priceless for many reasons. No one wants to feel

GO ON

alone or empty. Friends are always accepting, never questioning. They are always by your side no matter what. They can support you when you are down, or celebrate with you as you achieve your greatest victories. Choose your friends wisely, and do not forget how important they are to you.

1 Which of the following qualities may have been a reason why Buster was left at the pound so late in the day?

A. Buster was too excitable and a person may not want such an active dog.

B. Buster's small size may have left some people thinking he was unhealthy.

C. Buster was all the way at the end of the pound by himself, making someone believe he did not get along with other dogs.

D. Buster's cage already had an "adopted" sign on it.

2 Katie's morning started off with

A. having to prepare to go to Boston.

B. having to wake up even though she was trying to sleep.

C. remembering the great qualities of her dog.

D. remembering that she left her dog outside.

3 Buster came into Katie's life at a time of

A. great change.

B. complete happiness.

C. absolute misery.

D. overwhelming busyness.

4 In the 7th paragraph, the word **instantaneous** can be replaced by which of the following?

A. immediate

B. absolute

C. sudden

D. alarming

5 The overall message of this story is

A. people do not make as reliable pets as dogs.

B. if you take care of your pet, he or she will take care of you.

C. friendship should be valued in all its forms.

D. moving to a new place is not always easy.

GO ON

6 The following details from the passage are all evidence that Buster is a loyal friend except

   A. Buster would scratch at the inside of the apartment door whenever he would hear the jingling of her keys as she struggled to get them out of her pocketbook to unlock the door.

   B. when she was sick and feeling pathetic herself with the flu, Buster was by her side.

   C. with the clinking of his collar, this small, brown dog begins to make his trek to his owner's side.

   D. as soon as the door was opened an inch, he bolted in with a wag of his tail.

7 Which of the following statements best describes the relationship between Katie and Buster?

   A. Having been thrown together, both do their best to make it work.

   B. Each is continuously getting on the other's nerves.

   C. Each one seems to be an important part of the other's life.

   D. Both go about their lives independent of each other.

8 Buster can be described as all of the following except

   A. laid back.

   B. easy to get along with.

   C. tolerant.

   D. needy.

9 Based on the passage, what can make the process of going through a change easier?

   A. having a close friend go through it with you

   B. asking others to help you out

   C. buying things such as a pet

   D. taking time out of your schedule to do what you want and to relax

GO ON

10. Friends usually have characteristics in common with each other, but not always. What qualities do you feel are important in a friend? Do you think about those qualities when you are becoming a friend with someone?

Write your response in your answer booklet.

DO NOT GO ON
UNTIL YOU ARE
TOLD TO DO SO.

Day 2
Section 2

For the persuasive writing section of the test, you will have 45 minutes to complete your answer to the prompt. A space has been provided for you to use for prewriting and to organize your thoughts. Your prewriting WILL NOT be scored.

The part that will be scored will be your written response. Be careful not to write outside the box because any writing outside the box will not be scored. When you have completed your response, be sure to check over your work in this section only. Do not work on any other sections.

Once the 45 minutes is up, put your pencil down, and close your book.

The town council is considering adding a new housing development where a park is currently located. While the new houses would allow more people to move into the town and stop some of the overcrowding, it is the last piece of open grass and forest the town has.

The town council is interested in what the citizens of the community have to say on this issue. Write a letter to the mayor supporting the building of the new housing development or leaving the land as open space. In your letter, be sure to include examples and other evidence to support your decision.

GO ON

Prewriting:

_____

_____

_____

_____

_____

_____

_____

_____

_____

_____

_____

Write your response in your answer booklet.

DO NOT GO ON
UNTIL YOU ARE
TOLD TO DO SO.

Day 2
Section 3

You are now ready to begin Section 3 of the NJ ASK Language Arts Literacy test. You will have 30 minutes to complete the reading passage and the questions that follow. This section will include 9 multiple-choice questions and 1 open-ended response. Work up to the page that has the "stop sign" on the bottom or until time runs out.

If you finish early, check over your work. Remember, you may only check work in this section.

Destination: Discovery

Fred, a person who liked sleeping in his own bed, did not like hot temperatures, and did not know any other languages, was going to a small town in Italy for five weeks with his wife, Izzy. Izzy was Fred's complete opposite. She loved traveling and living in new places, spoke bits and pieces of various languages, and was just easygoing. How would these five weeks go? It was anyone's guess. It could be a miserable experience of "I told you so" and "Why did you even bother coming?" or it could be the time of their lives.

As the trip started, interesting was the only way to describe it. Izzy would be traveling with a group of musicians to attend some classes in how to speak Italian and sing opera. The airport was so crowded it was as if tickets were being given away for free. People were arriving from Philadelphia, New York City, and New Jersey all looking for their departures. Some were headed on weekend business trips, some were headed on family vacations to fun-filled beaches, and some were saying heartfelt good-byes as they were leaving a loved one to return home. Whatever the reason, complete strangers from all walks of life were being filtered into the same security and ticket lines.

The flight was scheduled to leave in an hour, so there was some time to kill. Fred, as usual, was hungry so he planned on getting something to eat. "Boneless Buffalo wings and French fries please," he ordered. He wondered to himself when the next time would be when he'd be able to order something like that. Izzy was wondering what the apartment would look like. She knew if it were not nice, it would be a long and miserable 5 weeks. She glanced over at Fred who was smiling as he enjoyed his delightful snack.

"Flight 509 to Bologna, now departing," the voice came over the loudspeaker. As the nine-hour flight left the ground, Fred was thinking that there was no turning back now just

GO ON

as Izzy was thinking how much she could not wait to get to their new home. For most of the flight, Izzy was reminding Fred that he needed to talk to people and that even though they did not know anybody, they would be spending five weeks with them so it would be nice to make friends. Fred was deep in thought reminiscing about his Buffalo wings and fries.

[5] After the flight, both of them were itching to get off the plane and stretch their legs. After getting their passports approved and retrieving their luggage, the adventure was under way. A day was going to be spent in the city of Bologna before heading to the small town of Urbania. After checking into the hotel, the sightseeing was about to get started. Fred was excited because even though he did not like living outside his comfort zone, he felt that maybe he should give this trip a chance. Izzy was just as excited because she was about to start practicing her Italian. The city was beautiful and historical in many ways. This happened to be the 4th of July as well. It was far from what they were used to. Being away from the United States, there were no barbeques or parties or baseball games, just life as usual.

The next day, after checking out of the hotel, they traveled back to the airport to take the group's bus to the small town. After arriving at the airport, Fred immediately spotted the group sprawled out across the area. Many of the travelers looked as organized as the inside of a tornado! Upon spotting the crowd, Izzy quickly remarked, "Remember, be nice."

The group was informed that the bus ride would be approximately 2 hours long. "Ugh," was the only sound that escaped Fred's mouth. As the bus got under way, Fred observed the surrounding landscape. He turned quickly to Izzy, "Izzy! You know I get bus sick right?" As the words came out of his mouth he noticed that Izzy was already fast asleep. Again, "Ugh" came out. Fred lowered his sunglasses and started listening to his music player trying to find his happy place.

When he lifted his sunglasses, he was amazed at the beauty of the area on both sides of the road. Trying to count the sunflowers in full bloom would be like trying to count the grains of sand on the beach. Finally, after what seemed like an endless stomach-wrenching bus trip, Urbania was reached. This was the definition of a small town. Everyone knew everyone else, there was one way in and one way out, and the whole town would meet in the town square every Thursday night!

As they were traveling into the town, Fred noticed a food store that looked quite interesting with a market outside. Since he loved to cook, he became rather excited. As the lethargic travelers stumbled off of the bus, Fred and Izzy noticed another couple. The husband came over to Fred and asked, "Excuse me, the song you were listening to on your music player, are you a fan of that band?"

GO ON

[10] "Am I a fan? I have seen them 12 times in concert! Are you kidding me? How about you?" eagerly asked Fred.

"Well, they do not come to Michigan a lot, but I have seen them 2 or 3 times." Fred was excited. He felt he had found a sense of normalcy in an area that was far from his comfort zone. Maybe Izzy did not have anything to worry about. Maybe Fred would have the time of his life on this extended trip. Who knows? Stranger things have happened.

1 How would you describe the relationship that Fred and Izzy have?

   A. They are opposites in every way imaginable and fight about what they do not agree on.

   B. They are opposite in many ways, but they do have some similarities.

   C. They are alike in many ways, but have some differences.

   D. They are almost identical and it is easy to see why they get along so well.

2 Why did Fred enjoy his airport meal so much?

   A. Fred ate two of his favorite foods.

   B. The meal was cooked to perfection.

   C. Fred was enjoying what he was comfortable with before leaving to see something new.

   D. The two travelers had been traveling all day and were looking for anything to eat because they were so hungry.

3 Why was the 4th of July such a unique experience for Fred and Izzy?

   A. This was the first year that Fred and Izzy spent traveling on this date.

   B. The festivities were like nothing they had ever seen before.

   C. As a result of the difference in cultures, there was no 4th of July celebration.

   D. Because Fred and Izzy were in a different country, there was not a 4th of July.

4 In Paragraph 8, "trying to count the sunflowers in full bloom would be like trying to count the grains of sand on the beach" means

   A. the sunflowers are too numerous to count.

   B. the sunflowers are small and too difficult to count.

   C. the sunflowers are all small and brownish or tan color like sand.

   D. the sunflowers are small and get lost in the landscape.

GO ON

5 In Paragraph 9, the word **lethargic** means

   A. unhappy.

   B. excited.

   C. energetic.

   D. exhausted.

6 The scene at the airport is included to

   A. show the reason why Fred does not like to travel.

   B. include an image of the diverse crowd that was gathered.

   C. show why Izzy was excited to travel.

   D. present the conflict that would occur in the story.

7 The theme or main idea of this story would <u>best</u> be described as

   A. opposites can attract.

   B. learning about new cultures can be a rewarding experience.

   C. trying something new might produce better results than just thinking you will not enjoy it.

   D. doing activities that you know you will like is the best way to get through life.

8 The writer's purpose in this passage was to

   A. persuade

   B. inform.

   C. entertain.

   D. compare and contrast.

9 Why did Fred feel that the 5 weeks would be better than he expected?

   A. A concert with his favorite band was announced.

   B. Fred was able to find a restaurant with his favorite food.

   C. Fred did not get too bus sick.

   D. Fred made some observations that this experience may not be too different than back home.

10 Based on the passage, explain why you feel Fred had the wrong idea entering this trip. What could he have done differently to have made his travels a better experience?

Write your response in your answer booklet.

DO NOT GO ON
UNTIL YOU ARE
TOLD TO DO SO.

Practice Test 1

Language Arts Literacy

Answer Key

Day 1

Section 1

1. B
2. D
3. A
4. D
5. C
6. A
7. B
8. D
9. B
10. See Detailed Explanations of Answers

Section 2

See Detailed Explanations of Answers

Section 3

1. D
2. C
3. D
4. B

5. C
6. D
7. B
8. D
9. A
10. See Detailed Explanations of Answers

Day 2

Section 1

1. C
2. B
3. A
4. D
5. C
6. D
7. A
8. C
9. A
10. See Detailed Explanations of Answers

Section 2

See Detailed Explanations of Answers

Section 3

1. C
2. A
3. B
4. D

5. C
6. D
7. C
8. B
9. A
10. See Detailed Explanations of Answers

Practice Test 1

Language Arts Literacy

Detailed Explanations of Answers

Day 1

Section 1

1. B

The best answer for this is *B*. After a long period of time, the penguins need to get food to replace the weight they lost. So *replenish* most closely means to "stock up on."

2. D

Since the penguins described in the story share parenting duties, they are comparable to the fox family. It is the only choice where the male and female both care for the babies.

3. A

While A, B, and C all present threats to penguins, A is the most severe. It is because the building of the hotel can wipe out the entire colony, not just 1 or 2 birds. D is not a threat because penguins do not live in the Northern Hemisphere.

4. D

Choices A and C have nothing to do with parenting. They only deal with why penguins are good underwater swimmers. Choice B is interesting, but does not explain why they are good parents. The feature of having the webbed feet to keep the egg off the cold ground is key.

5. C

Paragraph 7 deals with human dangers to penguins. Litter is man-made, so this that relates to the main idea of the paragraph.

6. A

Even though consistency can mean steadiness, it does not in this context. Remember to use your context clues and plug what you think is the definition into the sentence.

7. B

The author seems to focus on the protection of penguins in the final parts of the essay. So, B would make the most sense.

8. D

A through C are all individual parts that make up the passage, but D encompasses the meaning of the whole piece of writing.

9. B

While an encyclopedia may seem like a good choice, the passage does contain some opinions. Encyclopedias only contain factual information.

10. Penguins are much more suitable for underwater life than humans. The main reason for this is because penguins' bodies are built for swimming. The first difference can be seen by starting at the bottom of the body. Webbed feet act like mini-propellers, while human feet basically just kick around. Penguins can hold their breath with ease for a greater amount of time than humans. People often gasp for air just from swimming across a pool, but penguins emerge from even chilly waters effortlessly. Another reason penguins are built for swimming is their feathers. The feathers are a much warmer insulator than people's skin. Comparing the two, it is no wonder that penguins are much better swimmers than people.

Day 1

Section 2

The game "telephone" is one that many children enjoy playing. This game is when a person whispers something to one person. That person tells someone else, then that person tells someone, and it goes on until the message passes to everyone else in the room. The last person announces to the class what the message is. It is usually something completely different from the first message. While this is an amusing game to play, it is not as amusing as real-life situations of gossiping with its resulting hurt feelings.

An example of not talking directly to the person who said something can be seen by looking at a situation that happened recently in the girls' locker room. As some friends were preparing for gym class, they were calling themselves "losers" because of how bad they were at basketball. Another couple of girls were talking about going over to their friend Mary's house after school. Someone on the other side of the locker room heard the following, "Mary is a loser, and I will be seeing her after school!" That girl decided to tell Mary. Mary immediately asked, "What are they planning to do to me after school?" The other girl did not know and Mary panicked. Mary assumed that she was going to get beat up so she went to the principal. The principal called all the girls down, and by the time it was all sorted out, Mary felt extremely stupid. She did learn a valuable lesson, though. If she actually talked to any of the other girls herself, instead of listening to talk about what they said, she would have discovered there was absolutely nothing to worry about.

The second example occurred during softball tryouts. I was one of two sixth graders trying out. As I was walking down the hallway after the first day of practice, I heard some of the older girls commenting that the coach has never taken or will never take a sixth grader. I started to wonder why I was even trying out. When I told my Mom, she got angry and asked if I actually heard this from the coach or from the other girls. She made me go in early to talk to the coach the next morning. The coach was furious that the girls were spreading these rumors. She stated that she had not taken any sixth graders the past few years because they were not that good! She also told me that I better show up at tryouts that day! I felt so much better that I heard those words from the coach instead of believing the words a person spoke about her.

President Reagan was correct in saying that problems can be avoided as simply as just talking to another person. It is amazing how quickly a minor misunderstanding can escalate into a major problem. Just remember the next time you hear the words, "I heard," come from somebody's mouth, that they may not be entirely true. If you are concerned, go to the actual person and work things out.

Day 1

Section 3

1. D

This choice shows how much respect both boys had for their fathers because they treasured the gifts they received instead of going right out to spend it on something they wanted for themselves.

2. C

The moments described in the other choices were all experiences that left a memory for a positive reason. Being stuck in traffic does not show why someone should be grateful, but why they may have been upset not being where they were supposed to be.

3. D

The entire story traces the narrator's recollection of how an experience became important to him. As a young boy, he did not recognize the value of the gifts he received, but as a father he embraced all the stories and life experiences of his father and his grandfather.

4. B

The other children loved getting the coins as a present; however, the narrator did not appreciate the coin until after the moment. This, in fact, broke the cycle.

5. C

Use context clues from the paragraph to find out that the family has a lot of people without a lot of money. Because of this, new items are scarce.

6. D

The father was waiting for his son's fifth birthday to give him the coin. This can be inferred by previous information in the story. Missing out on giving someone a special gift would definitely make someone upset.

7. B

Choices C and D should be eliminated immediately. Even though much history happened during the time of the coins, each coin was a gift from a father to a son so there was a special link to one's own family and its history.

8. D

The narrator remembered how he tried to stay up for his father to arrive home for his birthday. Even though he was not angry, he probably was disappointed. He did not want to have his son feel disappointed in him.

9. A

Just reading the paragraph tells that the house was slightly chaotic with that many people trying to do a variety of activities.

10. Many times people think the best gifts are the ones that cost the most money. This is not always true. Sometimes the best gifts are cheap in price, but valuable in their meaning. When I was going on my first vacation without my parents I was nervous before I left. Even though I was going with my grandparents, it would be the longest amount of time I was away from home. My parents gave me a little stone with the word "love" carved in it before I left. Any time on that trip I missed them or wanted to go home, I would look at that stone and it would remind me of being home! It was great. I have brought that stone with me on every trip I have gone on since then. Just like the coins in the story, I could never sell the stone and get a lot of money for it, but it does have a sense of richness in my heart for what it represents.

Day 2

Section 1

1. C

The author never tells the reader which type of tank is better. Information is presented in a neutral, informative fashion.

2. B

The passage makes it clear that the tank should be set up well in advance of purchasing fish. This way, the owner can check the water to make sure it is consistent and can support the fish in a healthy way. The other choices may be good reasons, but they are minor compared to B.

3. A

C and D are not mentioned in the passage. The passage also does not compare fish to animals. Choice A presents a realistic picture of what fish ownership is like.

4. D

Temperature and the amount of salt in the water are responsibilities of saltwater fish. Choices A and B say that there is no difference between the 2 while C does not relate to the question.

5. C

The paragraph describing the tank remarks that there is no difference between a saltwater and freshwater tank.

6. D

All the other choices are exactly what you should pay attention to when taking care of a fish.

7. A

Since fish are used as pets, the need to have their diets closely watched is very important to the health of the fish. The other choices do not fit into the sentence.

8. C

The introduction and conclusion paint a clear picture that fish are alive and can be used to brighten up any room.

9. A

The other choices describe people who are extremely busy or young. The person who has weekends free will have time to care for the tank.

10. Both types of fish tanks present the owners with certain responsibilities. I would select a freshwater tank because it is easier to take care of. With fresh water, you don't have to constantly test the water. You just have to occasionally clean it. The fish also come in such a variety of colors that they are comparable to the salt water variety. So basically, you can get the same benefits without all the work. The food is not as specific either. The fish seem to be hardy and would have a better chance of surviving. Saltwater fish are more expensive and sensitive to change. Based on these reasons, I would select a freshwater tank.

Day 2

Section 2

Dear Vice Principal:

Discipline in the school is a huge problem! Students in the middle school are constantly getting in trouble and they are not concerned about the consequences. After-school detention does not seem to be regarded as a punishment, but more like a hangout session. These students need a more severe punishment to get them to follow the school rules. Saturday morning detention sessions may be the answer to this problem.

Having to go to school an extra day a week is much more severe than just staying after school. Having to wake up early an extra day would be extremely painful for a middle school student. "I hate waking up for school as it is. I cannot imagine having to wake up before 8 a.m. on the weekend. That is just mean! I definitely would listen to my teachers instead of doing that," commented Lawrence. This sixth day of school for rule breakers would definitely open some eyes and cause some students to reconsider their actions.

Also, a Saturday session is a good form of punishment because it requires a greater effort to actually show up at the detention. Currently, students just have to walk from their lockers down the hall to the main office. This walk to sit in the office really does not act as much of a deterrent. Having to get a ride to school on a Saturday morning requires much more of an effort. Parents will have to drive to the school to drop off and then pick up these students. This inconvenience might encourage parents to become more involved in changing their child's behavior.

Another benefit of a Saturday session is that the school can actually make use of the time it has with these rule breakers. While a principal or vice principal is often tied up with other activities at the school during the week, on a Saturday, the staff can spend time with these students. During this time, the staff can discuss what the students did that was wrong, why they did it, and how they can actually learn from their mistakes so they do not keep making them. This strategy has been tried in many neighboring schools and has reduced detentions by 25 percent! These lessons can actually be much more useful than just having a student sit there.

Saturday morning detentions are a great idea to try and improve student behavior. They will serve as a much more severe consequence than just having a student sit in the office after school. Not only will they serve as a consequence, but they can also serve as a valuable learning opportunity. The school should definitely look into these sessions as an effort to improve the behavior of students.

Day 2

Section 3

1. C

Even though the main character is pretending he is in a faraway place, he actually is just at school.

2. A

While the rest of the choices are all present somewhere in the text, they are not the main point of the story. Ernest's imagination gets him through the day at school, a place where he would obviously rather not be.

3. B

Since science fiction contains some very farfetched, imaginative ideas, Ernest would most likely enjoy that kind of reading.

4. D

The bus gave off a cloud of smoke as it was driven away. Looking at the choices and the context of the word, this is the only answer that would make sense.

5. C

While this is a somewhat tricky question, look at the choices carefully. D is not the best choice because teachers and students are not usually friends. In C, people who take the bus every day usually have some people they like to sit by and do not wish to be alone.

6. D

While Ernest is taking the time to study here, he is doing it late at night at the last minute. Even though he is getting his work done, it is not in an organized fashion.

7. C

The last two are the best choices; however, Ernest goes through his day on his own. The rest of the students barely whisper at him and the teacher just yells at him.

8. B

Pay attention to what is actually happening in the story and not in Ernest's mind. Think about your own classes. How do you feel when someone gives a seemingly endless list of things for you to do?

9. A

Ernest seems to hate school. That is why he creates such an elaborate story for himself to get through the day.

10. Imagination can be a powerful force in somebody's life. In the story, Ernest absolutely hates school. He only has one friend and his teacher has no patience for him. Getting through the day sounds like a painful experience for him. Being as young as he is, he needs to find something to make the day bearable. In this case, imagination helps him a lot. He has a friend, and seems to behave somewhat normally with him. He gets his work done, remembers to study, and is not a behavior problem. Ernest is not a bad kid, and it does not seem as if he would ever hurt anyone, so his imagination is not hurting him at all. He is making himself much happier by having this creative side. Sometimes living in a made-up world is much more enjoyable than living in the real world.

Practice Test 2

Language Arts Literacy

Answer Key

Day 1

Section 1

1. B
2. D
3. C
4. A
5. C
6. D
7. C
8. B
9. C
10. See Detailed Explanations
    of Answers

Section 2

See Detailed Explanations of Answers

Section 3

1. B
2. A
3. D
4. B

5. B
6. D
7. C
8. D
9. C
10. See Detailed Explanations
    of Answers

Day 2

Section 1

1. B
2. B
3. A
4. A
5. C
6. D
7. C
8. D
9. A
10. See Detailed Explanations
    of Answers

Section 2

See Detailed Explanations of Answers

Section 3

1. B
2. C
3. C

4. A
5. D
6. B
7. C
8. C
9. D
10. See Detailed Explanations of Answers

Practice Test 2

Language Arts Literacy

Detailed Explanations of Answers

Day 1

Section 1

1. B

Mr. Copperstein realized that all of his students were writing on topics that were not extremely newsworthy. They were just ordinary topics that people probably would not want to read about.

2. D

The scene was ominous for the girls because of the crows and stories they heard about the "Bird Man." The flowers were seen only after they entered later on in the story. The owner was not a criminal at all.

3. C

Looking at the section, Janet imagines a very elaborate story that focused on people paying attention to her.

4. A

Gossip happens throughout the story. By looking at the other choices, one can see that they do not have any evidence to support them throughout the passage.

5. C

By reading the text of the letter, the content showed more of a broken man than a dangerous one.

6. D

While all of the choices are valuable lessons to keep in mind for life in general, the theme of paying attention to a person's inner qualities instead of outward ones is found throughout the story.

7. C

Choices C and D should be the ones left after a quick read. By the tone of the letter, Paul does not seem excessively amused, but is inviting. If he wanted to know who found the hat, he would have to use the name the townspeople gave him so he could identify himself.

8. B

Paul kept the birds because he saw them as similar to himself. Crows are often seen as unwanted even when they are healthy. Paul wanted to care for them as he did not seem to have anyone to care for him.

9. C

By paying him a visit, he felt that someone from outside his fence related to him. Based on the story, it did not seem like visits occurred very often.

10. Paul was trying to let the girls know that even though the town considered him to be an outsider or a threat, he actually had something in common with the girls. Haley had lost her hat and did not know how to get it back. Paul lost his sense of belonging and did not know how to get *it* back. When both items were returned, the characters were more than happy. They both felt that they would never again see these things. It was like finding a lost treasure after many years of searching.

Section 2

A hero has many qualities that someone finds important and worthy of respect. Many times a hero is seen as being the best at what he or she does. However, two qualities that make for a hero are putting others before oneself and performing an action that may not be seen as popular, but right. Anyone who fits these qualities should be considered a hero.

Putting others before oneself is not an easy thing to do. Oftentimes, people enjoy doing what they find enjoyable and find it difficult to give that up. This quality is often seen with how parents deal with their children. Countless times, parents are seen sacrificing a vacation or a night out with friends to make sure they are in attendance at their son's or daughter's school event or helping them with homework. While this is an example that is frequent, this does not make it any less heroic. A more extreme example of this can be seen with firefighters. Their job is to put others' needs in front of their own as they rush into a burning building. Putting their life in jeopardy to protect someone they have never met is heroic as well.

Another quality is doing what is right, not just popular. An easy decision is to do what the whole crowd is doing because then a person can just become part of the crowd. While this can be an easy way out, it may not be a good choice. Being a leader and standing up for your personal values is in itself heroic. It is very easy to laugh at someone when a crowd is mocking them; however, it is much harder to befriend that person or tell the crowd to stop. When people do that, they often put themselves at risk for being mocked themselves. This reaction from the crowd is what makes this quality impressive.

Heroes do not always have to hit the farthest home runs or make the most money. Many times we are surrounded by heroes doing seemingly ordinary things. But for the people whose lives they touch, their actions are impressive indeed.

Section 3

1. B

Read the question carefully as it says "except." Having the separate leagues in the forties is a difference when compared to baseball of today.

2. A

The passage describes baseball with the nickname "national pastime" because it is extremely popular throughout the United States.

3. D

Use context clues from the entire paragraph to create your own definition before just looking at the choices.

4. B

Read the choices carefully as some may sound true until a more careful look. However, the part describing the history of the Yankees tells that they have been in New York from their beginnings.

5. B

While C may seem correct, if civil rights had not changed in the United States, all the technological advances would not matter. Different nations began to have the opportunity to root for players from their country when baseball opened its doors to diversity.

6. D

While A may seem correct, the author goes into detail in the story about how the fans are always returning. However, the main idea seems to be about how baseball reflects current events.

7. C

Context clues provide the answer to this.

8. D

Baseball did not have any control over the events surrounding World War II, but in the 1990s, it did have control over whether or not to strike.

9. C

By looking at the answer choices, the theme of the passage can be found. Even though it focuses on change, certain aspects of baseball and life do remain the same.

10. Even though change can be seen as negative, more often than not, it can be positive. If conditions always remained the same, nothing would ever get better. Baseball's changes showed that change can indeed be positive. When African Americans and multinational players were allowed into the Major Leagues, a sense of fairness and equality was achieved. That alone was a huge change that not only benefited the game, but also the country.

Day 2

Section 1

1. B

Usually when people are looking to get a new pet, they are looking for one that is healthy. Buster's small size may have left many of the people unsure about his health.

2. B

Katie was doing her best to ignore the alarm and her dog, but she had to get ready for the day against her wishes.

3. A

She was in a new city and at a new school. This showed that her life was in a period of change.

4. A

This choice is better than C because the word *sudden* gives the feeling of shock at having the unexpected happen. Since she was in a flashback, the change back to real life was immediate.

5. C

The entire passage is about the friendship between a dog and his owner. All the details support this main idea.

6. D

The rest of the choices show why Buster is a great friend, but D has nothing to do with friendship.

7. C

As evidenced by their great friendship, it seems like one cannot imagine living life without the other.

8. D

The other qualities are seen throughout the text. Even though he needs to go outside, he seems to be very self-sufficient.

9. A

The passage talks about the relationship between Katie and Buster and how special their friendship is. Answer A is the best choice.

10. Friends have some great qualities and that is part of what makes them friends. The qualities of trustworthiness and loyalty are two of the most important. A friend should be someone you can tell your problems to and not expect the whole world to know the next day. A friend is loyal if he or she sticks by your side even if things are not going well. While these qualities may be in the back of a person's mind when making friends, they almost have to be tested. They need to be tested over time because that is the only way to see if a friend will remain trustworthy and loyal.

Section 2

Dear Mayor:

Chirping birds, playing children, and open space—or—cars driving, people shouting, and people moving in? This is a decision that the town is currently facing in regards to the future of the park. While more housing can be beneficial in preventing overcrowding in some parts of the town, having an open area is just as, if not more, beneficial. Keeping the park will provide enjoyment for citizens of the town for many years to come.

Keeping the park as a park will provide an open area for animal life to live. The park currently serves as a home for a variety of animals. Deer, groundhogs, rabbits, cardinals, hawks, turtles, frogs, and fish all can be found throughout the park. Last year a pair of rare, at least in this area, American kestrels nested in the forest past the baseball fields. "Seeing the kestrels in the park was a terrific sight. Once they find a place to nest they often return for as many years as their nest location is there," commented Nicholas David, a local bird-watcher. As the home of many interesting animals, the park should be preserved for future generations to enjoy and have the opportunity to watch.

In addition to the animal life, the park is the perfect location for recreational activities. Last year, the park served as home field for soccer, baseball, softball, and football teams. Many joggers use the area as their track. Ice skaters sometimes have the opportunity to use the stream when it freezes over. So, the area is very much used. Many citizens use this location for exercise and enjoyment. If the park were to be closed, many citizens would not be able to participate in the activities they so often enjoy.

Finally, having an open space in a town is why many people have moved to the suburbs. Building on every bit of space will make some citizens unhappy. Ten-year resident, Katie Jean, exclaimed, "If I wanted to look out my window and see what my neighbors were doing, I would live in the city! I don't, though. I enjoy having a backyard and seeing some open areas like the park." Many other residents feel the same way. If many more houses are built, the town will have more people. If there are more people, simple tasks like going to the movies or shopping will become much more time consuming.

Building more houses in the park may sound like a great idea, but take the time to examine what will be lost. Animals call this area home, people use this area for a variety of activities, and it is just a great area to enjoy. Before you make your decision about what the town council wishes to do with the land, take a trip to the park one weekend and see all it has to offer.

Section 3

1. B

The focus of the answer needs to be that Fred and Izzy are opposites. The way they feel about different events clearly shows this. However, B is the choice because they do have some similarities like love of music as Izzy is going to study opera and Fred seems to love bands.

2. C

Fred was not looking forward to actually living in a foreign land, so he was trying to make every effort to regain the things he enjoyed before he went off.

3. C

Because the 4th of July celebrates American independence, it is not celebrated in Italy, but that does not mean there is not a 4th of July on the calendar.

4. A

A is better than C because if the sunflowers were too small, they would not have been visible from the bus.

5. D

After a lengthy flight the day before, and a bus trip that day, the travelers were tired.

6. B

The airport is used to describe the setting of the beginning of the trip. There were many different people going to many different places for a variety of reasons.

7. C

Izzy seemed to always be trying to remind Fred to give things a chance. This can be seen in her enthusiasm to travel and her encouraging of Fred to give people a chance.

8. C

Looking back at the lessons from Chapter 2, this is a story, not an article to give the reader factual information.

9. D

Fred observed the food store that about him, as well as another guy who had the same musical likes as he did.

10. Fred did have the wrong idea about the trip. Before the travel even started, he pretty much was seeing the trip as a miserable time. By going into something with a negative attitude, his vision would be clouded and might actually cause him to miss out on a lot of great things. Just because he was going to experience a different culture, it should not automatically be seen as a bad culture. Obviously, Fred does not like leaving his comfort zone, but once he did he appreciated his surroundings. If he had gone into the trip with that attitude, he probably would have had a better time from the start.

Practice Test 1

Language Arts Literacy

Answer Sheet

Day 1

Section 1

1. (A) (B) (C) (D)
2. (A) (B) (C) (D)
3. (A) (B) (C) (D)
4. (A) (B) (C) (D)
5. (A) (B) (C) (D)
6. (A) (B) (C) (D)
7. (A) (B) (C) (D)
8. (A) (B) (C) (D)
9. (A) (B) (C) (D)
10. _____

_____

_____

_____

_____

_____

_____

_____

Day 1

Section 2

_____
_____
_____
_____
_____
_____
_____
_____
_____
_____
_____
_____
_____
_____
_____
_____
_____
_____
_____
_____
_____
_____
_____
_____
_____

Day 1

Section 3

1. (A) (B) (C) (D)

2. (A) (B) (C) (D)

3. (A) (B) (C) (D)

4. (A) (B) (C) (D)

5. (A) (B) (C) (D)

6. (A) (B) (C) (D)

7. (A) (B) (C) (D)

8. (A) (B) (C) (D)

9. (A) (B) (C) (D)

10. _____

_____

_____

_____

_____

_____

_____

_____

_____

_____

_____

_____

_____

_____

_____

_____

_____

Day 2

Section 1

1. Ⓐ Ⓑ Ⓒ Ⓓ
2. Ⓐ Ⓑ Ⓒ Ⓓ
3. Ⓐ Ⓑ Ⓒ Ⓓ
4. Ⓐ Ⓑ Ⓒ Ⓓ
5. Ⓐ Ⓑ Ⓒ Ⓓ
6. Ⓐ Ⓑ Ⓒ Ⓓ
7. Ⓐ Ⓑ Ⓒ Ⓓ
8. Ⓐ Ⓑ Ⓒ Ⓓ
9. Ⓐ Ⓑ Ⓒ Ⓓ
10. _____

_____

_____

_____

_____

_____

_____

_____

_____

_____

_____

_____

_____

_____

_____

_____

_____

_____

Day 2

Section 2

Day 2

Section 3

1. Ⓐ Ⓑ Ⓒ Ⓓ

2. Ⓐ Ⓑ Ⓒ Ⓓ

3. Ⓐ Ⓑ Ⓒ Ⓓ

4. Ⓐ Ⓑ Ⓒ Ⓓ

5. Ⓐ Ⓑ Ⓒ Ⓓ

6. Ⓐ Ⓑ Ⓒ Ⓓ

7. Ⓐ Ⓑ Ⓒ Ⓓ

8. Ⓐ Ⓑ Ⓒ Ⓓ

9. Ⓐ Ⓑ Ⓒ Ⓓ

10. _____

_____

_____

_____

_____

_____

_____

_____

_____

_____

_____

_____

_____

_____

_____

_____

_____

Practice Test 2

Language Arts Literacy

Answer Sheet

Day 1

Section 1

1. Ⓐ Ⓑ Ⓒ Ⓓ
2. Ⓐ Ⓑ Ⓒ Ⓓ
3. Ⓐ Ⓑ Ⓒ Ⓓ
4. Ⓐ Ⓑ Ⓒ Ⓓ
5. Ⓐ Ⓑ Ⓒ Ⓓ
6. Ⓐ Ⓑ Ⓒ Ⓓ
7. Ⓐ Ⓑ Ⓒ Ⓓ
8. Ⓐ Ⓑ Ⓒ Ⓓ
9. Ⓐ Ⓑ Ⓒ Ⓓ
10. _____

_____

_____

_____

_____

_____

_____

_____

Day 1

Section 2

_____
_____
_____
_____
_____
_____
_____
_____
_____
_____
_____
_____
_____
_____
_____
_____
_____
_____
_____
_____
_____
_____
_____
_____
_____
_____
_____

Day 1

Section 3

1. Ⓐ Ⓑ Ⓒ Ⓓ

2. Ⓐ Ⓑ Ⓒ Ⓓ

3. Ⓐ Ⓑ Ⓒ Ⓓ

4. Ⓐ Ⓑ Ⓒ Ⓓ

5. Ⓐ Ⓑ Ⓒ Ⓓ

6. Ⓐ Ⓑ Ⓒ Ⓓ

7. Ⓐ Ⓑ Ⓒ Ⓓ

8. Ⓐ Ⓑ Ⓒ Ⓓ

9. Ⓐ Ⓑ Ⓒ Ⓓ

10. _____

_____

_____

_____

_____

_____

_____

_____

_____

_____

_____

_____

_____

_____

_____

_____

Day 2

Section 1

1. Ⓐ Ⓑ Ⓒ Ⓓ
2. Ⓐ Ⓑ Ⓒ Ⓓ
3. Ⓐ Ⓑ Ⓒ Ⓓ
4. Ⓐ Ⓑ Ⓒ Ⓓ
5. Ⓐ Ⓑ Ⓒ Ⓓ
6. Ⓐ Ⓑ Ⓒ Ⓓ
7. Ⓐ Ⓑ Ⓒ Ⓓ
8. Ⓐ Ⓑ Ⓒ Ⓓ
9. Ⓐ Ⓑ Ⓒ Ⓓ

10. _____

_____

_____

_____

_____

_____

_____

_____

_____

_____

_____

_____

_____

_____

_____

_____

Day 2

Section 2

Day 2

Section 3

1. Ⓐ Ⓑ Ⓒ Ⓓ

2. Ⓐ Ⓑ Ⓒ Ⓓ

3. Ⓐ Ⓑ Ⓒ Ⓓ

4. Ⓐ Ⓑ Ⓒ Ⓓ

5. Ⓐ Ⓑ Ⓒ Ⓓ

6. Ⓐ Ⓑ Ⓒ Ⓓ

7. Ⓐ Ⓑ Ⓒ Ⓓ

8. Ⓐ Ⓑ Ⓒ Ⓓ

9. Ⓐ Ⓑ Ⓒ Ⓓ

10. _____

_____

_____

_____

_____

_____

_____

_____

_____

_____

_____

_____

_____

_____

_____

_____

_____

_____

_____

Notes

Notes

Notes

Installing REA's TestWare®

System Requirements

Pentium 75 MHz (300 MHz recommended) or a higher or compatible processor; Microsoft Windows 98 or later; 64 MB available RAM; Internet Explorer 5.5 or higher.

Installation

1. Insert the NJ ASK6 Language Arts Literacy Assessment TestWare® CD-ROM into the CD-ROM drive.

2. If the installation doesn't begin automatically, from the Start Menu choose the RUN command. When the RUN dialog box appears, type d:\setup (where *d* is the letter of your CD-ROM drive) at the prompt and click ok.

3. The installation process will begin. A dialog box proposing the directory "Program Files\REA\NJASK6_LAL" will appear. If the name and location are suitable, click ok. If you wish to specify a different name or location, type it in and click ok.

4. Start the NJ ASK6 Language Arts Literacy Assessment TestWare® application by double-clicking on the icon.

REA's NJ ASK6 Language Arts Literacy Assessment TestWare® is **EASY** to **LEARN AND USE.** To achieve maximum benefits, we recommend that you take a few minutes to go through the on-screen tutorial on your computer. The "screen buttons" are also explained there to familiarize you with the program.

Technical Support

REA's TestWare® is backed by customer and technical support. For questions about **installation or operation of your software,** contact us at:

> **Research & Education Association**
> **Phone: (732) 819-8880 (9 a.m. to 5 p. m. ET, Monday–Friday)**
> **Fax: (732) 819-8808**
> **Website: www.rea.com**
> **E-mail: info@rea.com**

Note to Windows XP Users: In order for the TestWare® to function properly, please install and run the application under the same computer administrator-level user account. Installing the TestWare® as one user and running it as another could cause file-access path conflicts.